VERSATILE TEACHING METHODS

Inspiring educators, parents, and ed-tech professionals to think out of the box and make learning diverse for learners

AMJAD RAZAL

ISBN 979-8-89067-718-1

Contents

Gratitude

As I stand on the completion of this milestone in my life, the publication of "Versatile Teaching Methods," I find myself overwhelmed with profound gratitude for the unwavering love, care, and support that has shaped this journey from the very beginning. This book is a testament to the collective efforts of countless individuals who have touched my life in many ways that my words cannot fully express.

To my parents, the bedrock of my life and the source of my encouragement, I owe immeasurable gratitude. Your belief in my dreams, your support to my crazy decisions, and your relentless encouragement during moments of doubt have been the driving force behind my pursuit of excellence. Thank you for instilling in me the values of resilience and determination, and for being my pillars of strength through every twist and turn.

To my loving wife Hafeeza, whose love and faith in me have been a beacon of light during the tiring process of writing and shaping this book, *I cannot thank you enough.* Your patience, understanding, and nonstop support have given me the space to immerse myself in this project and bring it to fruition. Your belief in my vision and your constant words of encouragement have been the wind beneath my wings. Thank you for being a loving, caring, supportive life partner and giving me the space I need at home every day.

To my parents-in-law, for embracing me as your own and showering me with love, *thank you.* Especially to my Father-in-law who never doubted my skills and supported me during the hard times of COVID-19 lockdown, when I was struggling for months to get the job I needed. When my wife was anxious, he expressed his faith in me with his words. *'I know Amjad very well, he will definitely do something better in life,'* which gave me the emotional relief I needed.

To my former colleague Prabija Sarangi, who dedicated countless hours reviewing and providing invaluable feedback on the teaching ways when I was working for a record title. I am deeply grateful. Your keen insights and constructive criticism have enriched my approach, making it more meaningful and impactful.

I extend my heartfelt gratitude to Abdul Khalique sir from Mangalore, Karnataka *(who is* more than double *my age).* He is the most empathetic person I have ever met in my life, who heard from me about the book and within five minutes assured me of the sponsorship which made its publication possible. Your belief in the message of this work and your support in bringing it to a wider audience is deeply appreciated.

I am indebted to all the teachers, mentors, and educators who have crossed my path, each leaving an indelible mark on my approach to teaching and learning. Your collective influence has shaped me into the educator I am today, and I am honoured to carry forward your legacy through this book.

To my friends Abdul Bari for pushing me hard to start the record process and constantly checking with me on the progress each week, Shafaqath Ali Khan, Mohammed Mubeen and Mustafa Bin Khalid for encouraging and believing in my work.

To my colleagues who have been a constant source of encouragement and enthusiasm, thank you for your trust in my abilities.

Last but not least, I extend my gratitude to every reader who will embark on this engaging journey with "Versatile Teaching Methods." It is my sincerest hope that this book ignites the spark of versatility and inspiration in your hearts, leading to positive changes in the lives of countless students. From the depths of my heart, thank you for choosing this book.

With love and gratitude,

Amjad Razal

Note

Dear Readers,

Thank you for choosing this book. I believe that you are an educator, a parent, or an ed-tech professional who works in the development of content or curriculum for learners. I believe that you would like to make the teaching-learning process better for your learners. I appreciate your decision to buy this book. I guarantee you that this will be a good read for your learning.

The ways or teaching ideas mentioned in this book are carefully chosen. Some of them may make sense to you and some may not. I am open to receiving your feedback on it and would like to consider your suggestions and learn from you as well. Remember, this book is for your review. Anything you would feel will work better for your learners, apart from the ones mentioned in this book, you can add the same to the ways elaborated here.

The language used in this book is simple and conversational like; *I am talking to you, and you are listening to me,* so that anybody can grab this book and understand the message. I do not belong to Shakespeare's family. I believe that anything that is communicated in simple and plain language, reaches the heart and mind of the receiver. I am at the giving end of this book, and you are at the receiving end. I hope you will like the book. Well, I am not asking you to give a 5-star rating to this, on any platform you find it on. If you find it really appealing, I would be forever grateful to you.

Introduction to the book

During the year 2017-18...

I was working as a Principal at a school in Kannur, Kerala. While I was executing my duties, I visited Grade 4 to see the teaching-learning process. It was a science class. It was a routine classroom observation. I made my notes from the class using the observation sheet and requested the teacher to meet me in the office to receive feedback.

The teacher came to my office when she was totally free. I made her sit on the chair and started talking about my findings from the observation. I started with appreciation first, followed by the areas of improvement. This had been my regular practice as I wanted the teachers to listen carefully and strike a balance between appreciation and constructive criticism. Had I only spoken about the areas of improvement, the teacher would have either taken it negatively and felt embarrassed or paid less attention to the criticism and not worked on her improvement.

During the conversation, I uttered, *"any lesson can be taught in many different ways, you need to find better ways to teach that lesson."* As I said that statement, it stuck to my mind. While I was going back home, I kept thinking over it again and again. As I was practising integrating technology into all my work, I grabbed the laptop and started writing about what could be those different ways.

I needed a lesson to put my thoughts in one place. I selected a lesson from English as my previous role had been to tutor kids on languages, I felt I was pretty good at it as I could easily think of different ways of teaching a particular lesson. I chose *'simple present tense'* to be the topic and initiated the thought process.

At first, I was confused about how to follow up on bringing new ways. I googled- *a quick and time-saving thing to do*. But, after scrolling through several pages and links, I couldn't find anything relevant or close to my idea. I felt that I had exhausted my mind. Therefore, I closed the laptop and engaged in other evening activities.

The second day was Friday. I kept thinking about continuing the plan but couldn't do it.

On Saturday, the thought of continuing the plan didn't come at all. I had almost forgotten that I had an amazing idea.

The following week, I couldn't think about it and didn't even check anything related to the plan on Google as well.

It was on Sunday evening that I remembered it and I told myself, *"Why don't you try and find out, this is a game-changing idea that nobody would've thought of. If you can finish it, you'll be famous."* My mind started giving me imaginations of the fame I would receive and therefore be called a genius.

With that imagination, I grabbed the laptop again. My mind was ready for the process to begin and started giving me ideas on how to complete the task. I wrote some keywords to begin the plan and decided to think based on those keywords, to make the thought process right this time.

I chose the same lesson *'simple present tense.'.* One of the keywords was *'activity for learning.'* For the next five hours, I somehow completed 23 different ways of teaching simple present tense. I took this time to imagine the activity the students are engaged in and accept that activity only if I successfully imagine the students having good learning and engaging experience with that. Whenever I shortlisted a new idea, my mind had another question *"What would be another way of teaching it?"* This question kept bothering me so much that I could not sleep the entire night.

The next day, I felt so confident about the plan, without a second thought I exclaimed, *"Why not make it a hundred ways?"* In the beginning, I had no plan to go beyond twenty or thirty, as it was just to check whether this idea would work or not. Now, I was sitting in front of the laptop on the desk, sipping tea, feeling proud of myself. *"You are a genius, man."* I heard my inner voice. I was able to feel the blood flow in my brain and something strange was going on inside.

Using the same key words, I went on to cross fifty. At this time, I was extremely proud and happy about this new discovery. I couldn't sleep that night again as I was totally engrossed in the laptop and finally crossed the hundred mark. It was one of the most incredibly amazing nights of my life.

The next day, I reached a hundred and twenty-three ways of teaching simple present tense. I kept my laptop aside, prostrated, and thanked God for this opportunity or blessing. I felt that I had been chosen for this discovery which I could give to other teachers to bring a massive change in the teaching-learning processes at institutions.

It was time to analyse the thought process I was involved in. I knew from the beginning that many of these ways may not be relevant to some teachers. And some of the ways may not really work for certain people. To make it more relevant, I got an idea!

The next day, Tr. Rameesha visited my office with her lesson plans. As I could read the activities she planned for her students, I opened the document and started giving suggestions about how to teach it in different ways, analysing in my mind whether it could be applicable to other subjects or not. I gave fourteen or fifteen suggestions for a lesson, I looked at the teacher's eyes, which were in utter shock, *"What did he eat today in the morning? How is he even suggesting so many ways to teach this lesson."*

She went to the staffroom and narrated the experience she had with me. Out of curiosity, Tr. Rizwana appeared in front of me, holding her lesson plan and having a smile on her face. I repeated the same thing with her too. She was also in similar shock. She thanked me while leaving the office with a lot of confidence on her face, probably thinking, *"I am going to execute one of the suggestions to become the best teacher for this subject."*

Now, my curiosity wouldn't stop. I wanted to try new methods or ideas to identify even more ways of teaching any single lesson. Bingo! I got an idea. Why not use the dictionary?

"Dictionary? what will you do with it?" My mind pondered over it for a while.

Both an idea and confusion came along to trouble me even harder. I asked myself, *"How to use the dictionary to identify some more ways to teach a lesson?"* I decided that I would start with the first page and choose only those *action verbs* that can be turned into a learning activity. Therefore, I started with 'A,' from page number one, till I reached the last page of the dictionary. Naturally, these ideas and suggestions come to mind when you are constantly thinking about something passionately to do something with it. Our mind is capable of giving us solutions to the problems we are trying to solve, precisely not just one but many solutions so that we can try different approaches to finally come up with the right, relevant, and applicable solution.

When I looked at the list, I got more than six hundred and thirty-two verbs that can be used in designing the learning activity.

While I was suggesting to the teachers in their planning, I wanted to check with all the subjects and their lessons to have such maximum ways of learning. Therefore, this exercise with the dictionary which I completed in a couple of hours, offered me a plan to try each verb with the lessons from different subjects. I checked with different lessons and came to the conclusion that all these 600+ are not applicable to every lesson, because there is a difference between content, context, order of thinking involved with another subject, and a few other subject-specific limitations. I found these verbs as per my understanding. *Dear reader, if you are more imaginative and creative, you can even go to a bigger list of action verbs that could be turned into an engaging learning process. But before that, you need to be thorough with a few things which I'm elaborating on in detail in the next few pages.*

For the next few days, I didn't even continue this plan as I had other important tasks at school to complete. But I was constantly thinking about this new discovery and a totally new experience with the dictionary.

Fortunately, I had two guests visit my school, who were none other than the school Principal at one of the branches and the Secretary of the same group I was associated with. While having lunch with them, I couldn't control myself and I explained about my new discovery. I was mindful that I could not disclose everything as I had considered my fellow Principal to be equally competent. And like I had this feeling of fame in my imagination, I cannot see that it is gone to some other person who can just copy the idea and claim it as the result of his own creativity and I remain like a fool who revealed the entire story.

I remember when I was briefly explaining about the discovery, I didn't see any profound reaction from either of them. I began to think that maybe it was a stupid idea because when you see someone who is equally competent and not reacting to it, you will certainly have second thoughts. Again, I asked myself, *"What if he is not understanding right now, just by verbally listening to me and he needs to see those ways to comprehend it."* I decided to show him the document later and first make the discovery more appealing.

After a few days, while having lunch with the school manager of my branch, I told him briefly about it and his reaction shook me to the core and made me rethink everything I worked on, either to continue it or stop it completely. He stated, *'That's a genius idea, let's start training the teachers at other schools and collect good fees for the sessions. We can be rich together.'*

My mind said *"NO."* Now, I am not doing this for money. I do not want any money for this. The reason I started and completed it after millions of thoughts in my mind and spending a huge number of hours was not to do this for money. The imagination of fame had nothing to do with it. It was just a feeling, nothing serious.

So, I dropped the plan to publish it, indefinitely.

During the year 2020-21...

In March, the Prime Minister of India declared a total lockdown in the nation. Every single person was forced to sit at home. Going out was strictly banned except for emergency and essential needs.

I moved from Kerala in April 2019 to Hyderabad (my hometown) and joined an education management company in the senior leadership. On 16th March 2020 (not even a week before the national lockdown), I had an amazing interview with the senior manager at a big education company in Hyderabad and was about to receive the offer letter in a couple of days. The senior manager was so impressed with my conversation, he exclaimed, *'Your career is on the right track,'* while shaking my hand in the end. The HR told me that it is positive, and you'll be receiving the offer letter soon. With that in mind, I believed that everything is going to be great as I will be part of a multi-national company, that too in a senior-level leadership position. I couldn't control my happiness for the next few days.

Then, the national lockdown was announced. Everything vanished from my imagination. Every dream and hope shattered into pieces. When I tried reaching out to HR after a couple of months, I was told that the company is no longer hiring anybody for any level. I was disappointed.

Being home and doing nothing, I remembered the conversation I had with the senior manager. I had mentioned the discovery of teaching a lesson in many ways, which actually excited him. All these years, I didn't think about it at all. While I was on my way to the interview, I had to recall a few achievements just to impress the interviewer. This is how I was able to recall it and it was fresh in my mind for the next few days.

In May 2020, I resumed the plan of publishing it. But, where to publish and how? I got an idea! Why not claim this as a record!? Like Guinness World Records or Limca Book of Records - I could only think of these two big titles at that moment. I checked the details of the process and eligibility requirements. For the formal approach, I decided to pursue it meanwhile, targeting the Limca Book of Records first.

I made a video keeping myself in front of the camera and explaining the different ways of teaching simple present tense. The video was ready. I filled in the application and submitted it within a couple of hours. After a few weeks, I got a reply from one of their officials, *'We are sorry, we cannot accept this as a record title or claim.* Again, I was shattered from the inside.

"This is a stupid idea, which won't work, I said to myself.

After a few weeks, I reflected on the way I presented it. I found out the mistakes committed. After checking again, I got to know about the India Book of Records, which is under the Limca Book of Records itself. This time, I made a lesson plan using the same template that was used by teachers for planning their activities. With the video and a lesson plan, sticking only to twenty-five ways of teaching simple present tense, I filled in the application and submitted it. Little did I read about the entire process, but just sent whatever I felt was sufficient enough, just to give them an overall idea. But, that's not how things work at all times.

After a few weeks, I got constructive feedback from one of their officials, *'We are not able to understand the lesson as it is from English. We request you to select any lesson from Science or Math, make such ways and resubmit it.'* It felt good. But Math or Science is not my expertise. This was another challenge. So, I had to take a break here.

After 6 months, in January 2021, I resumed it as I had a life-line support. My wife, Hafeeza is an MSc Pure Mathematics Graduate from one of the esteemed institutions in Hyderabad. It took me many months to see my wife as the real support that I needed. I was really stupid for not recognising her in the first place. Sometimes, what we actually need is right in front of our eyes, but due to a lot of stress or challenges, we cannot see them. She carefully checked all the ways, discussed what is right and wrong and suggested how it can be right. Her feedback shaped my thought process even though we both had little hope with this crazy idea at that time.

I made more than a hundred ways in the lesson planning document but sent only seventy just to check whether it would be selected or not. This time, with lesson plans, and a very lengthy video of over eight or nine hours, I made a worksheet for each, as I had to put my imagination of the learning activity onto a piece of paper. Finally, the video was ready. Recording it was a good experience but editing for another seven to eight hours of video was basically very time-consuming. I ensured that I would give my best this time, and if I failed, I would close this down forever and if I succeeded, I would be proud of myself.

When the video was ready, I rechecked all the details of the process. Before initiating it, I had to have it reviewed by experts. It is always better to get many people to review your plans so that with much feedback, you will finally make some credible work out of it. I sent this to one of my former colleagues who was a Math teacher for Grades 9 – 10 at the school where I worked as a Principal. Prabija Sarangi went through each way and suggested necessary changes to make it more effective planning. I got it reviewed by my wife again, as she was constantly suggesting minor changes to make and validating in my approach from time to time. After the second review, I sent it to Mr. Fazal, a Govt School Principal in Maharashtra. I got his contact from one of the parents at my school back in Kerala, who is still a fan and a follower of my work. Within two days, I got the review.

I believed that now I was all set to submit the document. As for the process, I had to submit approval letters from Gazetted Officers. My father-in-law got one for me and another one was arranged by the same parent I had counted on previously.

Filled in the application, and submitted the document with all the worksheets attached and the video links. It took nearly two-three months for me. The application was submitted on 15th March 2021.

I didn't hear anything from the India Book of Records. So, I considered all the effort to go in vain. I made up my mind that if I fail this time, I will drop it and will never pursue it.

In April 2021, I got an email from the India Book of Records office.

Greetings from the India Book of Records!

Congratulations, your claim has been finalised as a record title, 'Maximum ways devised to teach a topic in Math'. We appreciate the effort and patience shown by you. Your skills have been acknowledged and as per the verification done by the Editorial Board of India Book of Records, only the best have been elected and approved by us.

Oh my God! What just happened?

Now, I am an India Book of Records title winner.

I was on cloud nine or any higher cloud known or unknown. I shared the news with my wife, and she started jumping on the floor with tears in her eyes. 'Ma Sha Allah! Ma Sha Allah! I am so so so happy and proud of you jaan!' She called and informed her parents, they were equally happy and proud. I came out of my room and informed my parents, they were extremely proud.

In May 2021, I got a package from the India Book of Records consisting of a medal, a certificate, and a few other stuff.

The same day, I posted it on LinkedIn, a social networking application that I had started to use frequently during the lockdown. Within a couple of hours, it went viral. More than a hundred thousand impressions, two thousand and three hundred plus likes, and hundreds of comments, only to congratulate me.

I read every single comment. And tried my best to reply to each one of them. Out of all, there was this comment: *'I would suggest you compile at least fifty ways and write a book on them which will become a good resource book for other teachers.'* With this, I got the idea to write a book. I guess this is the benefit of some social media platforms where you can find amazing ideas, productive tips, and professional suggestions to achieve your goals. There are people in different parts of the world who selflessly suggest ideas with their comments to help you shape your future or personality.

Why didn't I publish the book in the same year or in 2022? But why in 2023? It was because I was jobless for a few months and had been looking for work. It was such a horrible situation in the following year, I thought with this achievement at least I would get a decent job, but couldn't. People were excited to hear it from me but were reluctant to offer the job with the package I expected. I was ready for a lesser package too, just to meet the needs of my family, but even the lesser package was very high for certain organisations.

In September 2021, I got a job in Karnataka. The chairman of that group also insisted that I write a book and let the world know about the new discovery. But I was managing my work and life and continued to balance both for the next few months.

In the year 2023, I decided not to delay it as it may not sound relevant to educators soon, with a lot of revolution happening around in different industries. Artificial Intelligence is on another level. After witnessing the increase of AI-based services, I finally decided to challenge it and show the world what any human intelligence can do or is capable of doing. Human intelligence with the right use of artificial intelligence, the sky is not the limit. At last, artificial intelligence is just a tool.

I understand that this must be looking too lengthy for you now. I believe knowing the context of any new discovery is equally important to learning about what it has inside for the people.

Therefore, I started writing on 26th June 2023 at 07:31 pm and wrote the last word on 26th July at 01:45 am. It took me a month to decide what lessons I would be picking, and how simple I could present them, with sample worksheets. It would have taken just a week to complete the task, but I gave myself the time and space to think rigorously and work on it each day with consistency. It so happened that just to finalise two or three ways, I spent the weekends doing research and studying in-depth about the lessons I had picked.

Remember, these ways have been shortlisted while I was authoring the book. Like I said earlier, some of them may make sense to you and some may not. The idea behind this book is only to give you an *idea*. If you can get it, you can make even more effective ways which are better than mine. I truly believe you are more creative or innovative than me.

There are a few prerequisites for better understanding. It is necessary to read the ways with better contextual understanding. You can finish it first and then carefully analyse the rest of the book.

This book is not only for educators but also for parents who are aware of teaching-learning processes or at least can spend time tutoring their wards at home. It is also for professionals who work at education technology companies in the Curriculum or Content development department, who use creativity and innovative thinking to make the lessons impactful. It is also for professors and lecturers who work in higher education departments, educating graduates and postgraduates.

Pre-requisite# 1

'Bloom's taxonomy: a cognitive domain'

To enhance the teaching and learning process, educators employ various instructional strategies and frameworks. One such prominent framework is Bloom's Taxonomy. It provides a structured and direct approach to categorising educational objectives and guides the instructional process at institutions in any part of the world.

Origin of Bloom's Taxonomy: The development work of Bloom's Taxonomy can be traced back to the 1950s when Benjamin Bloom, along with his colleagues, sought to create a framework that would classify and promote different levels of cognitive thinking. Their objective was to move beyond traditional rote memorisation and encourage deeper understanding and application of knowledge. The taxonomy was first published in 1956 and has since undergone revisions and adaptations to better align with contemporary educational practices.

The Key Components of Bloom's Taxonomy: It consists of three main domains i.e., the cognitive, the affective, and the psychomotor. I am explaining the cognitive domain in brief as it is directly connected to the book.

a. The Cognitive Domain: This domain is divided into six hierarchical levels, each representing increasingly complex cognitive skills:

i. *Remembering*: This foundational level involves recalling or recognising information.

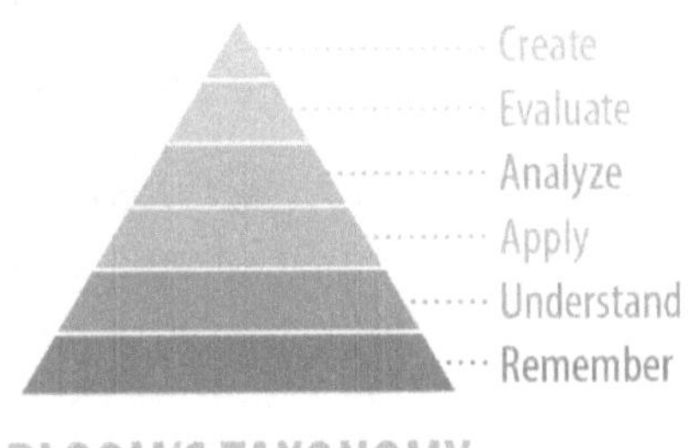

ii. *Understanding:* This level requires comprehension and interpretation of ideas or concepts.

iii. *Applying:* This level requires applying knowledge to real-world situations or solving problems is the primary focus of this level.

iv. *Analysing:* This level requires breaking down information into its constituent parts and examining relationships between them is the main objective here.

v. *Evaluating:* This level requires making judgements and assessments based on criteria and evidence.

vi. *Creating:* This level requires the highest level to encourage learners to generate new ideas, products, or solutions based on their understanding.

Each one of these levels has different verbs which are to involve the cognitive abilities of the learners. Each verb has to demonstrate the understanding that is taking place inside the learner's mind. Each level is connected to another level, expressing the growth of learning among the learners. Therefore, I take each verb and the level it is associated with seriously, to design the learning plan or growth for the learners. It serves as a valuable tool for educators in designing effective instruction, assessing the learning outcomes, and promoting higher-order thinking skills. There are some key reasons why Bloom's taxonomy is truly significant in education.

1. ***Clear learning objectives:*** Categorising learning objectives into hierarchical levels helps educators articulate specific and measurable goals. These goals help educators analyse the teaching-learning process and make necessary and immediate changes to make the learners learn better.

2. ***Curriculum development:*** It helps in structuring curriculum design by providing support for progressing from basic knowledge acquisition to advanced application and demonstration of knowledge, either in a visual or written form.

3. ***Instructional strategies:*** Educators can tailor their teaching strategies to match the desired cognitive level as per the needs

and capabilities of the learners. This facilitates the use of diverse instructional methods, such as questioning techniques, collaborative learning, and problem-solving activities.

4. ***Assessment design:*** It assists in creating assessments that evaluate the comprehension, critical thinking, and problem-solving abilities of each learner. It encourages the use of assessment methods that go beyond simple recall and promote deeper understanding. It also helps in designing different assessment formats for each learner as per his/her requirements.

5. ***Higher-Order Thinking skills:*** It stimulates critical thinking, creativity, and independent thought, essential for students' success in the 21st century.

6. ***Simplification of complexity:*** The hierarchical nature of Bloom's Taxonomy can help simplify the complexity of cognitive processes. When you see someone struggling with higher-order levels, you have to immediately go back to lower levels to make sure that they are thorough with all the lower levels and demonstrate mastery. When it is assured that they are now ready to go up, you must choose the higher ones by gradually taking the learners each level up with thorough practice. For this, I advise the educators to know each learner really well and their cognitive abilities.

7. ***Cultural and contextual differences:*** In a classroom full of learners from different backgrounds, especially at international levels where the learners are also from different nationalities, educators should consider adapting and contextualising the taxonomy to suit their specific needs and design the instructions in a way that it matches their needs.

8. ***Integration of domains:*** The cognitive, affective, and psychomotor domains are interconnected in real-world learning experiences. Bloom's Taxonomy focuses primarily on the cognitive domain, where it depends on the educators to integrate the other domains to help the learners get maximum time acquiring knowledge with the right blend of all domains, considering the other aspects of learning.

Pre-requisite# 2
'Imagination technique'

"Imagination is more important than knowledge." - Albert Einstein

"Imagination is the beginning of creation." - George Bernard Shaw

If you read the two quotes, there is one thing common between the two, i.e., imagination. I say, *'Imagination is the first stage of any change you'd want to make in your life or the world.'* For educators, it is one of the powerful techniques to design an effective learning activity for students. It helps educators identify the right activity, choose the right teaching-learning tools and materials, and disregard anything which doesn't fit in.

Let me put it in simple terms. We imagine as we read. We imagine as we speak or listen to the speaker. We imagine many things in a day and night. When you are getting bored while sitting in a lecture, your mind starts showing you images or flashes of past or future events or anything similar. When you are reading a book or a story, you see those characters in a visual form inside your mind, acting accordingly, as you read about their story. Similarly, when you are listening to the narration of a story, you start imagining those characters in your mind. This is a simple example of imagination.

We cannot stop ourselves from imagination. Our brain has been made to think and imagine. When you see a problem, your brain automatically shows you images to make things right or how they can be right. With imagination, learners are also given chances to think critically and identify the methods or ways to solve it. Innovators you come across use imagination to invent possible solutions across the world.

How did I learn to imagine? Let me take you back a little from 2023 to 2015.

I learned to imagine the activities from one of the eminent education leaders with whom I had an opportunity to work during my time in Kerala. She was the Principal of the school. While reading the lesson plans submitted by the teachers, she used to imagine the learning activity as it is written from the start to the end for a session of forty minutes and suggest what she thought was missing out. In the beginning, it was hard for me to imagine like she used to and decide for myself whether it would be effective or not. I used to simply write a plan and submit it assuming that my job was done. But I used to receive them back after her review with a lot of sketches on it, like a child playing with a pen and paper. After going through the same experience the following weeks, I instantly gave up. I went straight to the HR department and said, "This is not working out. I have a lot of work to do and the Principal is expecting me to redo the plans every single week. I went to meet Sharon Tabayag, a Philippine national appointed as the Cambridge Coordinator at the school and narrated the same thing. She replied, *'Why don't you check what you write and think whether this will work or not for your learners?'* I took her words seriously and tried to understand how the plans were being reviewed, and what is going on in the Principal's mind when she was checking all the lesson plans. I wanted to follow the same process and reduce the pain of redoing, reworking, and resubmitting it.

So, to plan any learning activity, I started to think about *i. how the activity is being introduced to the students, ii. how the instructions are being spoken, iii. how long are they taking to understand the instructions, iv. how they are initiating or taking part in the activity, v. how smooth is the activity going with all materials and tools taken to the class, vi. how each material or tool is helping the learners as per their needs, and vii. how they are ending it. And if there are two activities planned within a session, viii. How are they transitioning from one to another?*

To finalise one activity, I used to think again and again, take one or two hours to shortlist, design or customise it for the learners and finally mention that in the plan. After practising it for a few weeks, I eventually got the remark *'not bad'* without any more sketches or drawings. It gave me a sense of accomplishment. So, to plan activities for all the grades I had to teach, I used to spend two or three days of continuous thinking and imagination. Later, I made a checklist for myself to reduce the pain of the process, especially when it is a weekend and I have plans to hang out with friends at Kozhikode beach or have food at any restaurants within the city. I firmly believe the learning I had during those days with this experience, helped me when I became the Principal of a school to train the teachers in writing better lesson plans and also later when I was working on the record document.

If you are aiming to become one of the effective or best educators, before teaching the students, practising and planning the activities will help you in many ways.

Let me give another example here:

Think of a famous actor or movie star you admire the most. Imagine that he or she is with you right now. They are at your house in the drawing room with you. They are sitting on the sofa and listening to you. They are eating your favourite dish you cooked for them. They are hugging you as they depart from your house. *If you do not have any favourite movie actor, I will leave it to you to think of something, someone, or someplace you admire the most. Then, think of what kind of an experience you want in your imagination.* Every single line will make you imagine exactly in the same way as you read them, even though it never happened. This is the power of our brain, we can create any kind of imaginary experience we want with people, places, or things. *Please don't imagine hitting them.* ☺

Use this technique to plan your lessons. I did the same when I was working as an educator and when I was working on the record document. You can go back to the page where I mentioned that I scanned the entire dictionary to choose the verbs for the *cognitive process*, which to me is the *learning activity.* For each verb, I was imagining it as an engaging learning process. When I was able to see the right effect I needed, I chose them to be on the list, else rejected it.

Here is an exercise for you:

Imagine yourself doing the following actions. Read each statement, close your eyes if you want to and imagine the action associated with the verb. You can also keep your eyes open - if you can imagine successfully with your eyes wide open.

Reading a book	Watching the children in the garden	Climbing the stairs	Drinking mango juice
Sleeping on a couch	Watering the plants in the garden	Sitting on a bench	Walking on the road
Listening to your child	Jumping on floor	Writing a letter	Helping your friend
Dancing with your children	Eating food	Travelling in a car	Flying in an airplane

If you can do it successfully, for each statement given in the box, you can use this technique to plan the lessons and the learning activities for the learners.

Pre-requisite# 3

'Pre-reading the content before teaching'

I firmly believe that effective teaching requires careful preparation and a thorough understanding of the content being taught. Pre-reading lessons, where educators familiarise themselves with the materials before presenting them to students, play a vital role in ensuring high-quality instruction. There are a few benefits of pre-reading.

1. ***Comprehensive understanding of lesson content:*** Reading the content of the lesson in advance allows educators to develop a deeper and comprehensive understanding of the material. As they know their learners, it will give them a choice to make differentiation in the instruction that matches the needs of the learners. By immersing themselves in the subject matter, educators can:

   a. *Identify key concepts and objectives:* Pre-reading enables educators to identify the essential concepts, learning objectives, and main ideas of the lesson. And with the right understanding of the taxonomy, it allows educators to choose the right objectives as per the learners.

   b. *Get the context and connections:* Educators who read the content beforehand can appreciate the broader context of the lesson, including historical background, interdisciplinary connections, real-world applications or any subject-specific contextual facts and information. This perspective allows for more meaningful integration and relevant instruction.

   c. *Identify potential challenges:* Through pre-reading, educators can anticipate potential difficulties that students might encounter in understanding the content, depending on their cognitive requirements. This empowers educators to proactively plan instructional strategies and provide the necessary support to address student challenges effectively.

d. *Identify the right materials and tools*: Pre-reading allows educators to identify any materials or tools or resources that help in understanding the lesson.

2. ***Pedagogical preparation***: Pre-reading lessons support effective pedagogical preparation by empowering educators to:

   a. *Select appropriate teaching strategies:* Familiarity with the content enables educators to select suitable teaching strategies and instructional methods that align with the specific learning objectives as per the needs of their students. This preparation ensures that the chosen strategies effectively convey the content and engage learners.

   b. *Create engaging learning activities:* Pre-reading equips educators with the necessary knowledge to design engaging and interactive learning activities for different types of learners.

   c. *Plan assessments:* Understanding the content in advance allows educators to design assessments that accurately measure student learning outcomes. It helps educators align assessments with the lesson objectives, ensuring that students are assessed on the intended knowledge and skills.

   d. *Adapt instruction to individual needs*: Pre-reading lessons provide educators with insights into the diverse needs, interests, and learning styles of their students. Educators can adapt their instructional approaches and differentiate their teaching to cater to the different needs of individual learners.

3. ***Confidence and classroom management:*** Pre-reading the content beforehand enhances educators' confidence and classroom management abilities in the following ways:

   a. *Professional confidence:* Pre-reading lessons equip educators with the necessary knowledge and expertise to present the material confidently. Educators who are well-prepared and knowledgeable about the content express confidence, which positively impacts student perception and trust in their abilities as teachers. During any session, whenever any question is asked related to the topic, the educators can confidently answer any of them by making explicit links between the concepts.

b. *Smooth delivery:* Familiarity with the content ensures a smooth flow of instruction, minimising disruptions, and maintaining students' focus. Educators who have read the content in advance are better equipped to deliver clear explanations, answer questions effectively, and facilitate meaningful discussions.

c. *Flexibility and adaptability:* Pre-reading allows educators to anticipate potential challenges or questions that may arise during instruction. This preparation enables educators to think on their feet, adapt their teaching strategies in real-time, and address unexpected student inquiries or misconceptions effectively.

d. *Time management:* Educators who have pre-read the content are better equipped to allocate appropriate time for each section of the lesson. This helps them maintain a balanced pace and ensures that sufficient time is devoted to crucial concepts or complex ideas.

4. ***Student engagement and learning outcomes:*** Pre-reading lessons significantly contribute to increased student engagement and improved learning outcomes:

a. *Personalised instruction:* Pre-reading allows educators to design instruction to the specific needs and interests of their students. By anticipating potential student questions or challenges, educators can provide targeted explanations, examples, and supplementary materials that resonate with students and enhance their understanding.

b. *Enhancing discussion and participation:* Pre-reading enables educators to design thought-provoking questions and discussion points that encourage active participation and involve critical thinking. Engaging in meaningful discussion becomes easier when educators are well-versed in the content and can guide students effectively.

c. *Facilitating deeper understanding:* Educators who pre-read lessons can facilitate deeper understanding by providing additional context, examples, and real-world applications. This comprehensive understanding of the content enables educators to scaffold learning effectively, helping students make connections and apply knowledge in meaningful ways.

If you are planning to do something that I did, but you don't consider reading the content of the lesson before teaching it, you will eventually doubt the tips or learning given in this book. At the same time, you will have doubts about your teaching strategies too as you do not experience significant change among your learners in academics.

Pre-requisite# 4

'Knowing the needs of the learners'

One of the major challenges that many educators face in different parts of the world is their learners showing little or no interest in the lessons. The educators try their level best or go with new strategies, and they wish that could help them but sometimes it fails miserably. Why does that happen? Why do some of the students not show interest in the lessons?

If you are looking for the answer or if you are probably aware of it, it is because the lessons are taught to them in a way the educators decided to teach, not in a way the students wanted them, as per their needs. Those lessons are planned as per the teaching style, not as per the *learning style*. Therefore, the learning styles must be given preference and teaching styles must match the learning styles.

In any educational setting in any part of the world, learners possess unique learning styles that influence the way they perceive, process, and retain information. Recognising and accommodating these diverse learning styles is crucial for educators to promote effective learning and maximise student engagement. There are three primary learning styles: *auditory, visual,* and *kinesthetic.* How to teach these different kinds of learners has always been a challenging task for many educators. I believe the distinguished teachers can cater to each type of learner within the given time of their sessions.

1. ***Auditory Learners:*** These learners prefer learning through verbal instruction and sound-based stimuli. To effectively engage and support auditory learners, educators can employ the following strategies:

   a. *Verbal Instruction:* Offering simple and clear verbal academic instructions helps auditory learners grasp and process information effectively in their minds. Educators should articulate concepts, provide relevant explanations, and present information through lectures, discussions, and audio recordings.

b. *Classroom discussions:* Encouraging class discussions allows auditory learners to engage in dialogue, share ideas, and verbalise their understanding of the subject matter. This interactive approach facilitates deeper comprehension and retention.

c. *Audio materials:* Utilise audio materials such as recorded lectures, podcasts, or audiobooks, to provide additional auditory reinforcement. These resources cater specifically to auditory learners' preferences and can enhance their comprehension and learning experience.

d. *Oral presentations:* Assign oral presentations to auditory learners, as this allows them to express their understanding and communicate effectively. Presentations enable them to consolidate knowledge and practice public speaking skills.

e. *Group work and debates:* Engage auditory learners in collaborative activities such as group discussions, debates, or role-play exercises. These activities encourage active participation, promote critical thinking, and enhance oral communication skills.

Example of auditory learners: *When you visit Hyderabad, India and would like to visit Charminar which is quite far away from Rajiv Gandhi International Airport, you meet someone to ask for directions. What they do is tell you each point you need to cross, the diversions you need to make to finally arrive at the place. You hear it all from them, remember each statement, and finally reach the destination. If your preferred style is auditory, you will remember it as you hear it.*

1. **Visual Learners:** These learners rely on visual hints, images, and spatial representation to understand and process information effectively. Educators can employ various strategies to engage and support visual learners:

a. *Visual aids:* Incorporate visual aids such as charts, graphs, diagrams, and infographics to illustrate concepts and enhance visual learners' understanding. Visual representations provide clarity and facilitate information effectively.

b. *Graphic organisers:* Utilise graphic organisers, mind maps, or concept maps to visually represent relationships between ideas, helping visual learners grasp the connections and structure of the subject matter.

c. *Visual presentations:* Create visually appealing presentations with compelling images, videos, and multimedia elements. These visuals aid in capturing the visual learners' attention, enhancing comprehension, and reinforcing key concepts.

d. *Demonstrations and videos:* Conduct demonstrations or use educational videos to provide visual demonstrations of complex processes or procedures. Visual learners benefit from observing the practical application of concepts.

e. *Colour coding and highlighting:* Encourage visual learners to use colour coding and highlighting techniques to organise and emphasise key information in their notes or study materials. This visual organisation supports information recall.

Example of visual learners: *When you visit Hyderabad and would like to visit Charminar which is quite far away from Rajiv Gandhi International Airport, you meet someone to ask for directions or you do it yourself. What they do is to open the mobile phone application called Google Maps or you write it down on a piece of paper with lines, important landmarks on the way to keep track, etc. You see it all on the screen or a paper, remember everything visually and finally reach the destination. If your preferred style is visual, you will remember it as you see it.*

1. **Kinaesthetic learners:** These learners learn best through physical movement, hands-on experiences, and sensory engagement. To effectively engage and support kinaesthetic learners, educators can implement the following strategies:

a. *Hands-on activities:* Incorporate hands-on activities, experiments, or collaborative activities to provide kinaesthetic learners with tangible experiences. These activities allow them to actively engage with the subject matter, enhancing their understanding and retention.

b. *Role-playing and drama:* Encourage kinaesthetic learners to participate in role-playing activities or drama exercises. These activities involve physical movement, body language, and sensory engagement, enabling kinaesthetic learners to internalise concepts effectively.

c. *Manipulatives and models:* Provide manipulatives such as blocks, puzzles, or models, to facilitate kinaesthetic learning. These concrete objects allow kinaesthetic learners to explore and manipulate concepts, fostering deeper comprehension.

d. *Field trips and outdoor learning:* Organise field trips or outdoor learning experiences that enable kinaesthetic learners to engage with the environment and apply knowledge in real-world contexts. These experiences promote hands-on learning and connect classroom concepts to the outside world.

e. *Physical response techniques:* Incorporate physical response techniques, such as gestures, movements, or role-based actions, into learning activities. These techniques enable kinaesthetic learners to associate physical actions with abstract concepts, aiding in their understanding.

Example of kinaesthetic learners: *When you visit Hyderabad and would like to visit Charminar which is quite far away from Rajiv Gandhi International Airport, you meet someone to ask them to take you there. You get inside the vehicle and follow the way by noticing the important landmarks and you finally reach the destination.*

1. ***Integration and flexibility:*** Recognising that learners often possess a blend of learning styles, educators must integrate strategies that cater to multiple modalities and provide flexible learning environments. The following approaches promote inclusivity and address the needs of diverse learners:

a. *Multimodal instruction:* Combine auditory, visual, and kinaesthetic strategies to cater to different learning styles within a single lesson. Incorporate a variety of instructional methods, such as lectures, visual aids, hands-on activities, and discussions, to engage all learners.

b. *Differentiated instruction:* Differentiate instruction by providing multiple pathways for learning. Offer a range of activities and resources that allow learners to choose the mode that best suits their learning style, ensuring all students can engage with the content effectively.

c. *Individualised support:* Provide individualised support to address specific learning style preferences. Encourage students to communicate their preferences and collaborate with them to design personalised learning experiences that meet their needs.

d. *Reflective practices:* Regularly reflect on teaching methods and their effectiveness in meeting diverse learning styles. Get feedback from students and colleagues to gain insights into the impact of different strategies, and adjust instruction accordingly.

Another example: The practical session someone has in the Science lab. During the class, all the teacher does is, just throw every piece of information in a lecturing method, which mostly benefits the auditory learners. If the teacher uses images, graphs, models, or any other tools or resources, it mostly benefits the visual learners. If the teacher takes them to the lab and makes them practice with tools and resources, it benefits the kinaesthetic learners.

These three learning styles or preferences are found in each student, but one remains always dominant. In some cases, two may be dominant, but we can't simply state which one is dominant in which student. There are tests for this matter. With the result in hand, the discovery should set its course of action. For those educators who just started their teaching career, I advise you to take time, probably weeks or months, with your students, to know them personally before you start catering to their styles.

Use the given table to know how you can identify the learning styles. Remember, similar questionnaires are also made by prominent personalities and institutions in the world to make it simple and easy for anybody to know his/her own preferred learning style. The questions given for each learning style have been framed after reading each questionnaire designed by the aforementioned people. I have tried to make them simple or basic for your quick understanding. For a more in-depth understanding of identifying the learning styles, I advise you to contact them and get the help you require.

Auditory Style: Circle 'yes' or 'no' as per your personality or preference.		
Do you enjoy listening to lectures or podcasts?	Yes	No
Do you remember information better when it is explained to you verbally?	Yes	No
Do you find it helpful to discuss topics with others to enhance your understanding?	Yes	No
Are you good at remembering spoken instructions?	Yes	No
Do you prefer listening to audiobooks over reading printed books?	Yes	No
Do you prefer using mnemonic devices or rhymes to remember information?	Yes	No
Do you enjoy participating in group discussions or study groups?	Yes	No
Do you find it easy to recall information from a lecture or presentation?	Yes	No
Do you prefer listening to music while studying or working?	Yes	No
Do you remember details better when they are read aloud?	Yes	No
Do you find it helpful to read aloud when studying or reviewing?	Yes	No
Do you prefer using voice notes or recording lectures to review later?	Yes	No
Do you enjoy storytelling or listening to stories from others?	Yes	No
Do you like to discuss concepts and ideas with others to deepen your understanding?	Yes	No
Do you remember information better when you hear it multiple times?	Yes	No

a. *Count the number of (YES) you have circled.*

b. *Write the total number here:* _______________

Visual Style: Circle 'yes' or 'no' as per your personality or preference.		
Do you find it easier to learn from diagrams, charts, or visual aids?	Yes	No
Do you remember information better when it is presented in a visual format?	Yes	No
Do you enjoy using colour coding and highlighting when taking notes?	Yes	No
Are you drawn to visual arts, such as painting or photography?	Yes	No
Do you prefer reading printed materials rather than listening to audiobooks?	Yes	No
Do you enjoy creating and using flashcards for studying?	Yes	No
Do you remember information better when you visualise it in your mind?	Yes	No
Do you prefer watching videos or demonstrations to understand concepts?	Yes	No
Do you use mind maps or flowcharts to organise information?	Yes	No
Do you prefer to learn through reading and looking at images?	Yes	No
Do you prefer using graphs or charts to present data and information?	Yes	No
Do you find it helpful to visualise information as mental images or mental maps?	Yes	No
Do you enjoy watching educational documentaries or visual presentations?	Yes	No
Do you prefer reading instructions or directions rather than listening to them?	Yes	No
Do you remember details better when you see them in written form?	Yes	No

a. *Count the number of (YES) you have circled.*

b. *Write the total number here:* ___________________

Kinaesthetic Style: Circle 'yes' or 'no' as per your personality or preference.		
Do you like to learn through hands-on activities and experiments?	Yes	No
Do you find it challenging to sit still for long periods?	Yes	No
Do you enjoy physical activities such as sports or dance?	Yes	No
Do you learn better by doing rather than listening or watching?	Yes	No
Do you use gestures or body movements while speaking or explaining something?	Yes	No
Do you like to take breaks and move around while studying or working?	Yes	No
Do you prefer activities that involve physical manipulation, like building models or crafts?	Yes	No
Do you find it helpful to act out scenarios to understand complex ideas?	Yes	No
Do you enjoy participating in role-playing activities or simulations?	Yes	No
Do you use physical gestures while explaining something to someone?	Yes	No
Do you prefer field trips or practical experiences to learn about new subjects?	Yes	No
Do you enjoy using hands-on materials, like manipulatives or models, for learning?	Yes	No
Do you find it helpful to take notes or draw diagrams to understand concepts better?	Yes	No
Do you enjoy experimenting and learning through trial and error?	Yes	No
Do you remember information better when you physically engage with it?	Yes	No

    a. *Count the number of (YES) you have circled.*

    b. *Write the total number here:* _______________

Write score of Auditory style: ______________, Visual style: ______________, and Kinesthetic style: ______________. Whichever style you find dominating, that is your preferred learning style.

Apart from different learning styles, identifying the learner's needs is equally important. It is fundamental to creating an inclusive and supportive learning environment. Their needs encompass various aspects, including academic, emotional, social, and physical dimensions.

1. ***Academic needs:*** It refers to the specific requirements learners have to achieve their learning goals. Addressing these needs is crucial for promoting academic growth and success. Key strategies for meeting learners' academic needs include:

    a. *Individualised learning plans:* Develop individualised learning plans or goals for learners based on their specific strengths, weaknesses, and areas of interest. These plans provide a roadmap for personalised learning and enable educators to track progress effectively.

    b. *Scaffolding:* Provide appropriate support and guidance to help learners build upon their existing knowledge and skills. Scaffolding techniques, such as breaking down complex tasks, modelling, and providing step-by-step guidance, assist learners in acquiring new concepts and abilities.

    c. *Individualised formative assessment:* Regularly assess learners' progress through individualised formative assessment strategies, such as quizzes, observations, or informal check-ins. Summative assessment can be done for the whole class at regular intervals. Formative assessment can also be made for the whole class when there is a similar pattern or style of learning among all the learners in the classroom. Whatever feedback you receive, it allows you to address areas of weakness and provide targeted support.

2. ***Emotional and social needs:*** It encompasses learners' well-being, self-esteem, and their sense of belonging and connectedness within the learning community. Recognising these needs contributes

to a positive and supportive learning environment. Strategies for meeting learners' emotional and social needs include:

a. *Building positive relationships:* Fostering positive and trusting relationships between educators and learners helps create a safe and inclusive space where learners feel valued, supported, and comfortable expressing their thoughts and emotions. *"How well connected am I to the learners?"* and *"What do I do to connect to them?"* Such questions must have positive answers to start building relationships between the two.

b. *Social-Emotional Learning (SEL):* Integrate SEL practices into the curriculum to promote emotional intelligence, self-awareness, empathy, and social skills. Explicitly teach and model these skills daily to enhance learners' emotional well-being and their ability to navigate social interactions.

c. *Active listening and empathy:* Practice active listening and demonstrate empathy towards learners' emotions, concerns, and experiences. Show genuine interest in their well-being and provide opportunities for them to express themselves.

d. *Peer collaboration and group work:* Foster opportunities for peer collaboration and group work to enhance learners' social skills, communication, and teamwork. Encourage learners to interact, share ideas, and support one another, fostering a sense of community and collective learning.

e. ***Physical Needs:*** It encompasses the requirements for a comfortable and supportive learning environment that helps learners' health and well-being. Recognising learners' physical needs is vital for promoting focus, engagement, and overall well-being. Strategies for meeting learners' physical needs include:

f. *Classroom environment:* Ensure that the classroom environment is clean, well-organised, and free from distractions. Consider factors such as lighting, temperature, seating arrangements, ventilation, and access to necessary resources and materials.

g. *Incorporating movement breaks:* Allow for regular movement breaks during longer instructional periods. These breaks help learners stay energised, promote circulation, and enhance focus and concentration. This is one of the reasons why there is a mandatory break after every two hours of continuous sessions at any standard school. You cannot just make the kids sit in one room for four or five hours without any break, which will only lead to the downfall of academic growth.

h. *Healthy habits:* Encourage healthy habits, such as proper nutrition, hydration, and regular physical activity. Educators can integrate discussions and activities on healthy lifestyles to reinforce the importance of physical well-being.

3. ***Cultural and Linguistic Needs:*** Cultural and linguistic needs encompass learners' diverse cultural backgrounds, languages, and experiences. Addressing these needs promotes inclusivity, cultural competence, and equitable education. Strategies for meeting cultural and linguistic needs include:

a. *Culturally Responsive Teaching:* Incorporate culturally responsive teaching practices that value and integrate learners' diverse cultural backgrounds and experiences into the curriculum. Use culturally relevant materials, examples, and perspectives to make connections and foster a sense of belonging.

b. *Multilingual Support:* Provide support for learners who are non-native English speakers or have multilingual backgrounds. This support may include bilingual materials, language support services, or peer support systems.

c. *Flexible Assessments:* Offer flexible assessments that accommodate diverse cultural and linguistic backgrounds. Consider alternative assessment methods that allow learners to demonstrate their understanding in different ways, such as through visuals, presentations, or portfolios.

d. *Inclusive Classroom Environment:* Foster an inclusive classroom environment where learners feel respected and valued regardless of their cultural or linguistic backgrounds. Encourage the sharing of diverse perspectives, experiences, and languages within the learning community through collaboration between the learners.

e. *Professional Development:* Engage in ongoing professional development to enhance cultural competence and understanding. Educators should continuously strive to expand their knowledge and skills in addressing the cultural and linguistic needs of their learners.

Pre-requisite# 5
'Learning Objectives'

Learning objectives form the backbone of any instructional design, providing a clear roadmap for teaching and learning. They articulate what learners are expected to know, understand, and be able to do by the end of a learning experience. They provide a clear focus and guide educators in planning instruction, designing assessments, and evaluating learning outcomes. They also outline the knowledge, skills, and attitudes that learners should acquire and demonstrate.

It is not just a statement that anybody can simply scribble. So what should a learning objective look like? What is called a learning objective? What is the structure of it? These days most of the curriculum designers and academic publishers mention the objectives in the book itself, making it easier for the educators to understand them and plan their lessons. There are some teacher guides that also specify how the learning process should be. Many educators use those guides as resource books, in which they find what they need. I will mention the structure of the learning objective, but before that I need you to understand the characteristics of an objective.

Clear:	It should be clear and concise, leaving no space for confusion or misinterpretation. It should specify the expected goal in a manner that is easily understood by educators, learners, and other stakeholders.
Measurable:	It should be measurable, enabling educators to assess learners' attainment of the desired goals. The use of action verbs facilitates the creation or demonstration of measurable learning objectives that can be assessed through various assessment methods.

Relevant:	It should align with the overall goals and standards of the educational programme or curriculum. It should be relevant to the subject area, age appropriateness, and the specific needs and interests of the learners.
Progressive:	It should be sequenced or structured in a way that reflects the progression of learning. It can build upon previously acquired knowledge and skills, guiding learners towards higher levels of understanding and proficiency.
Specific:	It should be specific, indicating the precise knowledge or skills that learners are expected to acquire. Vague or overly general objectives may lead to confusion and hinder effective instructional planning.

Examples of learning objectives across different domains of taxonomy: Learning objectives can be crafted for various domains, such as cognitive, affective, and psychomotor. Here are examples of learning objectives across different subject areas:

a. ***Cognitive Domain:***

    i. *Mathematics*: Solve quadratic equations by factoring and using the quadratic formula.

    ii. *Science*: Demonstrate an understanding of the scientific method by designing and conducting a controlled experiment.

    iii. *History:* Analyse primary and secondary sources to construct an evidence-based argument about a historical event.

    iv. *Language Arts:* Write an essay that supports a specific viewpoint using evidence and logical reasoning.

b. ***Affective Domain:***

    i. *Social-emotional learning:* Demonstrate empathy by actively listening and responding to a peer's concerns.

    ii. *Character Education:* Apply the principles of fairness, respect, and integrity in everyday interactions with peers and adults.

    iii. *Citizenship:* Participate in community service activities to develop a sense of social responsibility and civic engagement.

c. ***Psychomotor Domain:***

  i. *Physical Education*: Demonstrate proper technique and form in playing a football game.

  ii. *Fine Arts:* Create a sculpture using clay, incorporating various sculpting techniques and principles of design.

  iii. *Technology*: Develop a functional website that incorporates interactive features and user-friendly navigation.

Constructing effective learning objectives: Creating effective learning objectives involves a systematic process that aligns with the desired outcomes. The following **ISSR** steps can guide educators in constructing impactful learning objectives:

a. *Identify the desired outcome:* Determine the knowledge, skills, or attitudes that learners should acquire or demonstrate by the end of the learning experience. Consider the subject area, curriculum goals, and learners' needs.

b. *Select action verbs:* Select a relevant action verb from any of the six levels of the taxonomy or any action verb you can imagine, that could define or associate with the learning process which will eventually reflect the intended learning outcome.

c. *Specify conditions and criteria*: Describe any specific conditions or criteria under which the learning should occur or be evaluated. For example, time constraints, available resources, or level of complexity.

d. *Review and refine:* Review the learning objectives to ensure they are clear, measurable, and aligned with the desired outcomes. Seek feedback from colleagues or instructional designers, refining the objectives as necessary.

Structure of a learning objective:

Structure = [**condition**] [**target audience**] will be able to [**action verb**] [**knowledge**] [**measure of success**]
E.g.: **By the end of the session**, the **learners** will be able to **differentiate** between **2D and 3D shapes** with an **accuracy of over 90%**.

It depends on the educators, and how they articulate the objectives for the learners. They have flexibility here to just mention the *'condition,'* *'target audience,'* *'action verb*,' and *'knowledge*.' The measure of success varies from subject to subject, based on the context.

Furthermore, if I break it down to a simple level, each learning objective mainly consists of a *'condition,'* *'target audience,'* *'verb,'* and *'noun.'* *'Verb' defines the cognitive process and 'Noun' defines the type of knowledge.*

Pre-requisite #6

'Knowledge'

As per the book '*A taxonomy for learning, teaching, and assessing*' abridged edition by David Krathwohl and Lorin W. Anderson (2001), 'Knowledge' has been categorised into four types i. Factual knowledge, ii. Conceptual knowledge, iii. Procedural Knowledge, and iv. Metacognitive Knowledge.

1. **Factual knowledge:** It deals with information, truths, and concrete data about the world. It consists of facts and details that can be observed, measured, or documented, and it forms the basis for understanding various subjects and phenomena. Factual knowledge is essential for building a solid foundation of understanding and is often acquired through direct observation, research, education, and reliable sources of information. Examples:

   a. *Science: water boils at 100 degrees Celsius*

   b. *Mathematics: The sum of angles in a triangle is 180 degrees.*

   c. *Technology: The Central Processing Unit (CPU) is responsible for executing instructions.*

   d. *History: India gained independence in 1947 on 15th August.*

   e. *Geography: Charminar is the landmark of Hyderabad, Telangana.*

2. **Conceptual knowledge:** It deals with ideas, theories, principles, and mental representations of categories or concepts. Unlike factual knowledge which focuses on specific details and observable facts, conceptual knowledge is more abstract and generalisable. It involves understanding the relationships and connections between different elements to form a coherent framework of knowledge. Examples:

   a. *Mathematics: Understanding the concept of infinity.*

   b. *Science: Understanding the concept of evolution by Charles Darwin.*

c. *Psychology: Understanding Sigmund Freud's psychoanalytic theory, which explores the influence of the unconscious mind on behaviour.*

3. **Procedural knowledge:** It deals with the step-by-step processes, skills, and techniques required to perform tasks or solve specific problems. It is often referred to as "know-how" or "knowledge of how to do something." Unlike conceptual knowledge, which focuses on understanding ideas and principles, procedural knowledge is about practical application and action. Examples:

   a. *Driving: Understanding how to operate a vehicle safely and efficiently such as starting the engine, changing gears, using turn signals, and parallel parking.*

   b. *Cooking: Understanding the specific steps and techniques to cook dishes - such as knowing when to add ingredients, stirring, taking precise actions, etc.*

4. **Metacognitive knowledge:** relates to an individual's awareness and understanding of their own cognitive processes. It involves knowing how one learns, thinks, and solves problems. Essentially, metacognitive knowledge is about "thinking about thinking" and being conscious of one's own mental activities. This self-awareness allows individuals to monitor and regulate their cognitive processes, leading to more effective learning, problem-solving, and decision-making. Examples:

   a. *Problem-solving: Understanding how to find a solution to any problem by utilising all cognitive abilities.*

Pre-requisite #7
'Grouping Configuration'

It is a technique to make the teaching-learning process organised during instructional activities. Teachers can use different grouping configurations to enhance learning experiences to promote collaboration catering to individual needs. Better use of grouping configurations can produce a more engaging and supportive learning environment for students.

Here are some grouping configurations and ways to make better use of them while teaching:

1. *Whole Class Instruction:* The teacher addresses the entire class as a single group.

   - It is ideal for introducing new concepts, providing essential information, or setting the stage for a lesson.

   - Teachers can make better use of it by using multimedia, visual aids, and interactive activities to keep the students engaged during whole-class sessions.

   - It will help in encouraging questions and discussions to foster critical thinking.

2. *Small Group Collaboration:* Students are divided into small groups of 3 to 5 members.

   - It is suitable for problem-solving activities, discussions, and group projects.

   - Teachers can make better use of it by assigning roles within each group, ensuring equal participation, and providing clear instructions for the task at hand.

   - It promotes teamwork and helps students learn from each other.

3. ***Pair Work:*** Students work in pairs, often for specific tasks or discussions.

    • It is suitable for sharing ideas, practising communication skills, and gaining confidence.

    • Teachers can make better use of it by pairing students to encourage active listening and providing constructive feedback guidelines.

    • It boosts students' confidence and can create a comfortable space for shy learners.

4. ***Independent or Individual Work:*** Students work individually on assignments or tasks.

    • It is suitable for self-paced learning and building individual skills, as some students prefer to learn by themselves.

    • Teachers can make better use of it by offering a variety of activities to cater to different learning styles and abilities.

    • It provides clear instructions and ensures students have the necessary resources to work independently.

Pre-requisite #8
'Teaching Aids'

Teaching aids, tools, and resources play a crucial role in enhancing the teaching and learning process. Without the aids or tools or resources, the teaching will not have any measurable impact on their learning. They can make complex concepts simple, increase engagement, and cater to diverse learning styles.

Here are some commonly used teaching aids, tools, and resources and ways to make better use of them while teaching:

1. *Visual Aids:* These include posters, charts, diagrams, infographics, and multimedia presentations.

   - They are effective for presenting information, illustrating complex ideas, and supporting retention.

   - Teachers can make better use of visual aids by ensuring they are clear, well-designed, and relevant to the topic.

   - They can incorporate proper colour and images to make them visually appealing.

2. *Interactive Whiteboards or Smart TVs:* These allow teachers to project digital content and engage with it using touch or stylus input.

   - They enhance active learning, encourage student participation, and facilitate dynamic presentations.

   - Teachers can make better use of interactive whiteboards by preparing interactive lessons that involve students in problem-solving, dragging and dropping activities, and collaborative brainstorming.

3. ***Educational Videos:*** These can be pre-recorded lectures, documentaries, or animated explanations.

   - They offer a multisensory learning experience and cater to visual and auditory learners.

   - Teachers can make better use of educational videos by selecting high-quality content that aligns with the learning objectives.

4. ***Manipulatives:*** These are physical objects or materials that students can handle and interact with to understand abstract concepts.

   - They are particularly useful in mathematics, science, and early childhood education. Visit any Play School, you will find a good amount of manipulatives arranged in each room.

   - Teachers can make better use of manipulatives by incorporating hands-on activities that allow students to explore and experiment with the concepts.

5. ***Audio Materials:*** These include podcasts, audiobooks, educational songs, and recorded lectures.

   - They cater to auditory learners and can be utilised for on-the-go learning.

   - Teachers can make better use of audio materials by providing accompanying visual cues, summaries, or transcripts to support comprehension.

A Quick Note:

To give you an idea of how versatile teaching methods can be made, I picked two lessons from Grade 6 Science and Grade 5 Mathematics NCERT textbooks one from each. I made a sample of 25 ways of teaching each lesson. These are sample ideas for you. Each went through my imagination process and I am confident that they will work for the students or class I have imagined. I had made a huge list of versatile ways but shortlisted only 25 to not make this book thicker.

I believe that with the given ways, you will get an idea of how to make different learning activities for the same lesson. As you are about to read it for the first time, they might confuse you. You may think that these don't make any sense at all and all look the same. Well, they are the same because the lesson is the same. The way the lesson is being taught has a different level of cognitive abilities.

Before you read each way, here is something to remember.

1. Recall the prerequisites for your reference.

2. Each lesson plan targets a different cognitive process. From the list I made, I went on to imagine the way I want my learners to engage in, described it in a simple way for your understanding and easy reference. Remember, any lesson plan you read in the next pages is just a sample. It could be used as it is if it meets the desired expectation for the learning activity.

3. I made a checklist for each lesson plan so you can immediately check whether it is making sense or not.

4. I made a sample worksheet to give you an idea about how I want the learners to engage in the learning activity. Remember, any worksheet you see is just a sample for reference, not the exact one.

5. I made a checklist for each worksheet so you can immediately check whether it is supporting the learning activity or not.

6. During my thought process for each lesson plan, I may have gone too far in planning about teaching the content, but I made sure to stick to the particular grade level's cognitive complexity of the content. Even then, if you find anything irrelevant, remember point no. 2.

7. You may find that I have taken the planning from lower-order thinking skills to higher-order thinking skills. And somewhere, I brought in a lower-order thinking plan in between. I request you to excuse me for that as it's not about the flow here in all these ways. It is about involving a particular cognitive process when teaching a particular part of the content.

8. All the pictures or images are taken from online sources. If you own the image, please excuse me for that too. I used it only for the sample, not to claim that I'm the rightful owner or have the right to use it.

9. If you would like to suggest anything or give feedback, I have given my contact details at the end of the book. I'm looking

forward to receiving your valuable input about the book. *If you do, that's how I will gain an opportunity to learn from you!*

10. For each lesson, I have given a QR Code for you to carefully read through the content. Later, look at the sample lesson plans and worksheets to analyse them thoroughly.

Lesson #1 "Electricity and Circuits"

Subject: Science

This lesson has been taken from Grade 6 NCERT Textbook.

Scan this QR Code to read content of the lesson.

Plan #1	
Learning objective:	To accurately recall and articulate key principles, components, and applications of electricity, showcasing their comprehensive knowledge and retention of the subject matter.
Taxonomy level:	Remembering
Summary of activity:	Begin the lesson by asking students what they know about electricity. Explain that electricity is required to power many devices and appliances to function. Give each student a worksheet with two columns "Things that require electricity" and "Things that don't require electricity." Ask them to make a list and write them in respective columns. Ask students to share some examples from each category and explain why they fall into the respective category. Summarise the main points of the lesson by emphasising the importance of electricity.
Grouping configuration:	Individual – students will be made to sit individually, use the given worksheet, and complete the task.
Teaching aids/ tools/resources:	Worksheet

Checklist:

1. Is the planned activity aligned with the learning objective of the lesson?

2. Is the learning activity consisting of conceptual or real-life connections that will help the students understand its relevance and importance?

3. Is the learning activity suitable for small groups or the whole-class or for individual students?

4. Is the learning activity providing opportunities for engaging in conceptual understanding?

5. Is the learning activity inclusive of opportunities for students to reflect on their learning and make connections to prior knowledge and experience?

6. Is the learning activity accommodating the different ability levels of the students in the classroom?

If you marked [Yes] more than 5 from the above list, it simply means that the activity planned will work for the students.

Worksheet/ Engagement Idea # 1:

List out the things that need electricity.	List out the things that don't need electricity.
1. _______________	1. _______________
2. _______________	2. _______________
3. _______________	3. _______________
4. _______________	4. _______________
5. _______________	5. _______________
6. _______________	6. _______________
7. _______________	7. _______________
8. _______________	8. _______________
9. _______________	9. _______________
10. _______________	10. _______________

Checklist:

1. Is the worksheet aligned with the learning objective?

2. Is the worksheet aligned with the lesson plan covering the relevant concept?

3. Is the worksheet clear, concise, and easy for students to understand or use?

4. Is the worksheet allowing the students to develop their understanding of the concept?

5. Is the worksheet incorporating conceptual or real-life connection examples that students can easily relate to?

6. Is the worksheet designed to be completed in a given timeframe of the session?

If you marked [Yes] more than 5 from the above list, it simply means that the worksheet will help the students acquire the knowledge.

Plan #2	
Learning objective:	To define and articulate the diverse purposes and applications of electricity in various contexts. To explore and describe how electricity powers everyday devices, enables technological advancements and supports critical infrastructures.
Taxonomy level:	Remembering
Summary of activity:	Begin the lesson by asking students what they know about the uses of electricity. Make groups of students and ask them to brainstorm as many different purposes of electricity as they can think of. Ask each group to share their list of purposes of electricity. Write their responses on the board by categorising them as per their application. Give each student a worksheet and summarise the concept with some more explanation.
Grouping configuration:	Students will be divided into small groups to discuss the different purposes of electricity with peers and complete the given task.
Teaching aids/ tools/resources:	Worksheet, Pictures

Checklist:

1. Is the planned activity aligned with the learning objective of the lesson?

2. Is the learning activity consisting of conceptual or real-life connections that will help the students understand its relevance and importance?

3. Is the learning activity working for small groups or as a whole-class activity or individually?

4. Is the learning activity providing opportunities for engaging in conceptual understanding?

5. Is the learning activity inclusive of opportunities for students to reflect on their learning and make connections to prior knowledge and experience?

6. Is the learning activity accommodating the different ability levels of the students in the classroom?

If you marked [Yes] more than 5 from the above list, it simply means that the activity planned will work for the students.

Worksheet/ Engagement Idea #2:

Look at the images given below and write the accurate purpose of electricity for them.

Checklist:

1. Is the worksheet aligned with the learning objective?

2. Is the worksheet aligned with the lesson plan covering the relevant concept?

3. Is the worksheet clear, concise, and easy for students to understand or use?

4. Is the worksheet allowing the students to develop their understanding of the concept?

5. Is the worksheet incorporating conceptual or real-life connection examples that students can easily relate to?

6. Is the worksheet designed to be completed in each timeframe of the session?

If you marked [Yes] more than 5 from the above list, it simply means that the worksheet will help students acquire the knowledge.

Plan #3	
Learning objective:	To identify conductive and non-conductive pathways to develop a clear understanding of the flow of electricity.
Taxonomy level:	Remembering
Summary of activity:	Begin the lesson by asking students what they know about the things in which electricity flows and things in which it doesn't flow. Make groups of students, and ask them to brainstorm as many different things as they can think of in which the electricity flows (conductors) and doesn't flow (insulators). Ask each student in the group to use the worksheet to choose their options for both categories. Write their responses on the board for both categories. Ask the students to summarise the concept. End the lesson with some more explanation.
Grouping configuration:	Group - students will be divided into small groups to discuss the different purposes of electricity with peers and complete the given task.
Teaching aids/ tools/ resources:	Worksheet, Pictures.

Checklist:

1. Is the planned activity aligned with the learning objective of the lesson?

2. Is the learning activity consisting of conceptual or real-life connections that will help the students understand its relevance and importance?

3. Is the learning activity working for small groups or as a whole-class activity or individually?

4. Is the learning activity providing opportunities for engaging in conceptual understanding?

5. Is the learning activity inclusive of opportunities for students to reflect on their learning and make connections to prior knowledge and experience?

6. Is the learning activity accommodating the different ability levels of the students in the classroom?

If you marked [Yes] for more than 5 from the above list, it simply means that the activity planned will work for the students.

Worksheet/ Engagement Idea #3:

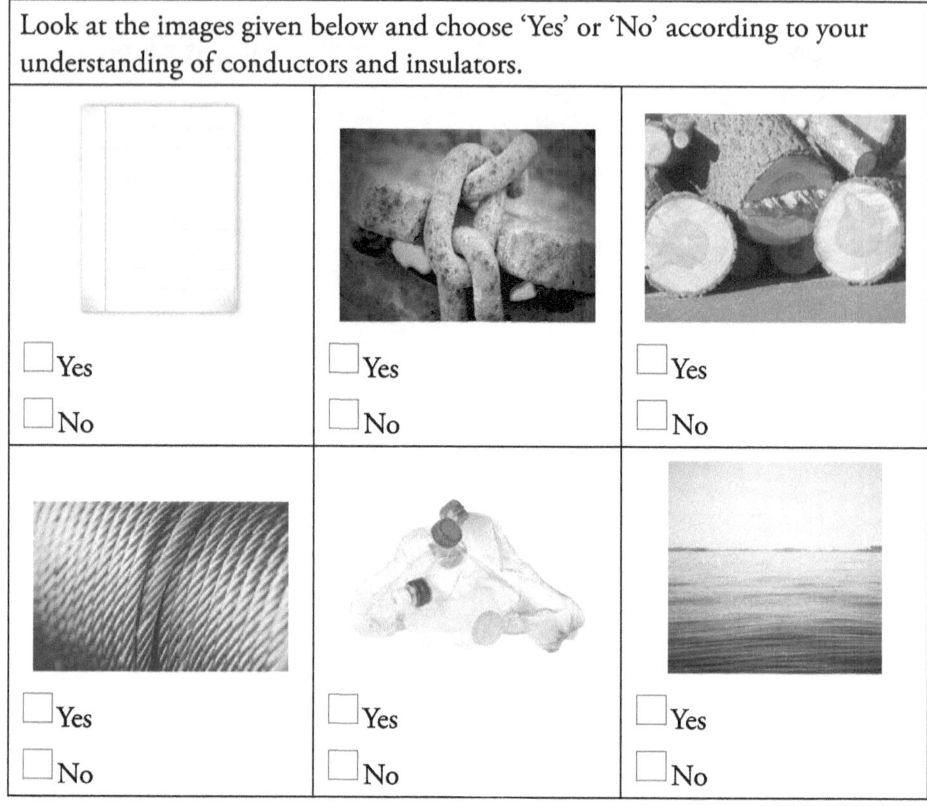

Look at the images given below and choose 'Yes' or 'No' according to your understanding of conductors and insulators.

Checklist:

1. Is the worksheet aligned with the learning objective?

2. Is the worksheet aligned with the lesson plan covering the relevant concept?

3. Is the worksheet clear, concise, and easy for students to understand or use?

4. Is the worksheet allowing the students to develop their understanding of the concept?

5. Is the worksheet incorporating conceptual or real-life connection examples that students can easily relate to?

6. Is the worksheet designed to be completed in each timeframe of the session?

If you marked [Yes] for more than 5 from the above list, it simply means that the worksheet will help students acquire the knowledge.

Plan #4	
Learning objective:	To accurately label and differentiate between various types of wires commonly used in electrical circuits. To get familiar with the properties, applications, and safety considerations associated with different wire types, to make informed decisions when selecting and utilising wires in electrical projects.
Taxonomy level:	Remembering
Summary of activity:	Begin the lesson by asking students what they know about the different purposes of electricity. Make groups of students and ask them to brainstorm as many different wires as they can think of or that they have seen anywhere in their house or locality. Ask each student in the group to take the wires provided and label each one of them as per their understanding and where they are used. Ask the students to summarise the concept. End the lesson with some more explanation.
Grouping configuration:	Group - they will be divided into small groups of 5 members each. They will be asked to look at the wires, label them and mention their uses.
Teaching aids/ tools/ resources:	Different types of wires

Checklist:

1. Is the planned activity aligned with the learning objective of the lesson?

2. Is the learning activity consisting of conceptual or real-life connections that will help the students understand its relevance and importance?

3. Is the learning activity working for small groups or as a whole-class activity or individually?

4. Is the learning activity providing opportunities for engaging in conceptual understanding?

5. Is the learning activity inclusive of opportunities for students to reflect on their learning and make connections to prior knowledge and experience?

6. Is the learning activity accommodating the different ability levels of the students in the classroom?

If you marked [Yes] for more than 5 from the above list, it simply means that the activity planned will work for the students.

Worksheet/ Engagement Idea #4:

Look at the images given below and label the wires according to your understanding.

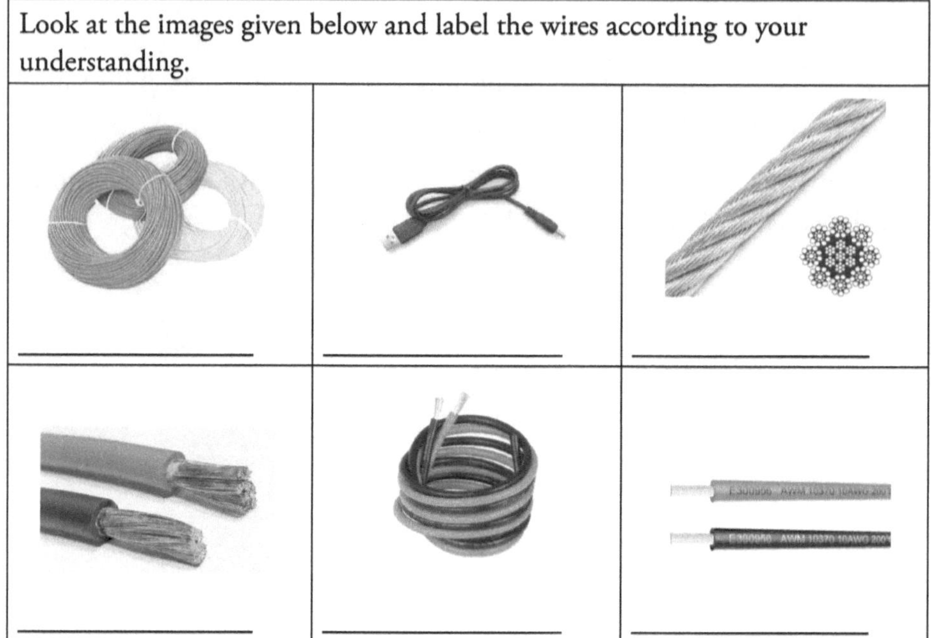

Checklist:

1. Is the engagement idea aligned with the learning objective?

2. Is the engagement idea aligned with the lesson plan covering the relevant concept?

3. Is the engagement idea clear, concise, and easy for students to understand or use?

4. Is the engagement idea allowing the students to develop their understanding of the concept?

5. Is the engagement idea incorporating conceptual or real-life connection examples that students can easily relate to?

6. Is the engagement idea designed to be completed in the given timeframe of the session?

If you marked [Yes] for more than 5 from the above list, it simply means that the idea will help students acquire the knowledge.

Plan #5	
Learning objective:	To define and describe various sources of energy used for producing electricity by exploring and articulating the characteristics, availability, environmental implications, and technological applications of different energy sources.
Taxonomy level:	Remembering
Summary of activity:	Begin the lesson by asking students what they know about the different sources of electricity. Make groups of students and ask them to brainstorm as many different sources as they can think of. Ask each student in the group to present the different sources of energy they listed out and define their purpose. Summarise the topic with some more explanation.
Grouping configuration:	Group - they will be divided into small groups of 5 members each. They will be asked to look at the pictures, name them and define their purposes.
Teaching aids/ tools/ resources:	Worksheet

Checklist:

1. Is the planned activity aligned with the learning objective of the lesson?

2. Is the learning activity consisting of conceptual or real-life connections that will help the students understand its relevance and importance?

3. Is the learning activity working for small groups or as a whole-class activity or individually?

4. Is the learning activity providing opportunities for engaging in conceptual understanding?

5. Is the learning activity inclusive of opportunities for students to reflect on their learning and make connections to prior knowledge and experience?

6. Is the learning activity accommodating the different ability levels of the students in the classroom?

If you marked [Yes] for more than 5 from the above list, it simply means that the activity planned will work for the students.

Worksheet/ Engagement Idea #5:

Look at the images given below and name the source of energy according to your understanding.

Checklist:

1. Is the worksheet aligned with the learning objective?

2. Is the worksheet aligned with the lesson plan covering the relevant concept?

3. Is the worksheet clear, concise, and easy for students to understand or use?

4. Is the worksheet allowing the students to develop their understanding of the concept?

5. Is the worksheet incorporating conceptual or real-life connection examples that students can easily relate to?

6. Is the worksheet designed to be completed in a given timeframe of the session?

If you marked [Yes] for more than 5 from the above list, it simply means that the worksheet will help the students acquire the knowledge.

Plan #6	
Learning objective:	To compare and contrast two or three different sources of energy used for generating electricity by exploring the advantages, disadvantages, environmental impacts, and sustainability aspects of each energy source.
Taxonomy level:	Understanding
Summary of activity:	Begin the lesson by asking students what they know about the different sources of energy. Make groups of students, ask them to brainstorm on two or three sources of energy, identify the similarities and differences between each and write them down in the worksheet. Ask each student in the group to present three or more similarities and differences of each source of energy. Summarise the topic with some more explanation.
Grouping configuration:	Group - they will be divided into small groups of 5 members each. They will be asked to look at the pictures and identify the similarities and differences between them.
Teaching aids/ tools/ resources:	Worksheet, Pictures.

Checklist:

1. Is the planned activity aligned with the learning objective of the lesson?

2. Is the learning activity consisting of conceptual or real-life connections that will help the students understand its relevance and importance?

3. Is the learning activity working for small groups or as a whole-class activity or individually?

4. Is the learning activity providing opportunities for engaging in conceptual understanding?

5. Is the learning activity inclusive of opportunities for students to reflect on their learning and make connections to prior knowledge and experience?

6. Is the learning activity accommodating the different ability levels of the students in the classroom?

If you marked [Yes] for more than 5 from the above list, it simply means that the activity planned will work for the students.

Worksheet/ Engagement Idea #6:

Look at the images given below and write the similarities and differences between each, according to your understanding.

Checklist:

1. Is the worksheet aligned with the learning objective?

2. Is the worksheet aligned with the lesson plan covering the relevant concept?

3. Is the worksheet clear, concise, and easy for students to understand or use?

4. Is the worksheet allowing the students to develop their understanding of the concept?

5. Is the worksheet incorporating conceptual or real-life connection examples that students can easily relate to?

6. Is the worksheet designed to be completed in a given timeframe of the session?

If you marked [Yes] more than 5 from the above list, it simply means that the worksheet will help the students acquire the knowledge.

Plan #7	
Learning objective:	To identify and differentiate between various components and symbols used in circuit diagrams, enabling them to interpret and create circuit diagrams accurately.
Taxonomy level:	Understanding
Summary of activity:	Begin the lesson by asking students what they know about electric circuits. Use the circuit diagram to explain each component and symbol. Explain how they function and what are their primary and secondary purposes. Ask each student to use the worksheet and match the following options. Make students retell the functions of each component and symbol. Summarise the topic with some more explanation.
Grouping configuration:	Individual – each student will be given a worksheet. They will be asked to recall and match the components and symbols correctly.
Teaching aids/ tools/ resources:	Worksheet

Checklist:

1. Is the planned activity aligned with the learning objective of the lesson?

2. Is the learning activity consisting of conceptual or real-life connections that will help the students understand its relevance and importance?

3. Is the learning activity working for small groups or as a whole-class activity or individually?

4. Is the learning activity providing opportunities for engaging in conceptual understanding?

5. Is the learning activity inclusive of opportunities for students to reflect on their learning and make connections to prior knowledge and experience?

6. Is the learning activity accommodating the different ability levels of the students in the classroom?

If you marked [Yes] for more than 5 from the above list, it simply means that the activity planned will work for the students.

Worksheet/ Engagement Idea #7:

Look at the symbols given below and match them to the components they represent.	
Symbols	Components
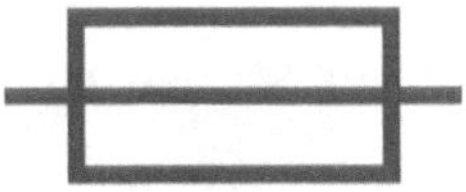	Power supply
	Bulb
	Cell
	Fuse
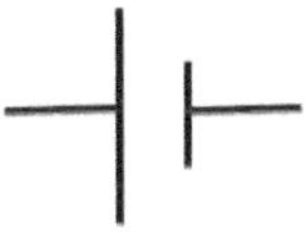	Ammeter

Checklist:

1. Is the worksheet aligned with the learning objective?
2. Is the worksheet aligned with the lesson plan covering the relevant concept?
3. Is the worksheet clear, concise, and easy for students to understand or use?
4. Is the worksheet allowing the students to develop their understanding of the concept?

5. Is the worksheet incorporating conceptual or real-life connection examples that students can easily relate to?

6. Is the worksheet designed to be completed in a given timeframe of the session?

If you marked [Yes] for more than 5 from the above list, it simply means that the worksheet will help the students acquire the knowledge.

Plan #8	
Learning objective:	To understand the functioning of electric cells and their applications in powering various electrical devices.
Taxonomy level:	Understanding
Summary of activity:	Begin the lesson by asking students what they know about the battery cell and its uses, depending on the sizes. Give each student the parts of a battery cell. Take one battery, open it up and show how it has been assembled. Ask each student to name the different parts of a battery and use the materials to assemble it, like a company-made battery. Use the materials to check whether they can generate electricity. Summarise the topic with some more explanation.
Grouping configuration:	Group - they will be divided into small groups of 5 members each. They will be asked to look at the pictures and identify the similarities and differences between them.
Teaching aids/ tools/ resources:	Worksheet, Parts of a battery cell, Wires, Digital multimeter (electricity checking device).

Checklist:

1. Is the planned activity aligned with the learning objective of the lesson?

2. Is the learning activity consisting of conceptual or real-life connections that will help the students understand its relevance and importance?

3. Is the learning activity working for small groups or as a whole-class activity or individually?

4. Is the learning activity providing opportunities for engaging in conceptual understanding?

5. Is the learning activity inclusive of opportunities for students to reflect on their learning and make connections to prior knowledge and experience?

6. Is the learning activity accommodating the different ability levels of the students in the classroom?

If you marked [Yes] for more than 5 from the above list, it simply means that the activity planned will work for the students.

Worksheet/ Engagement Idea #8:

Look at the images given below and name each part of the battery cell.

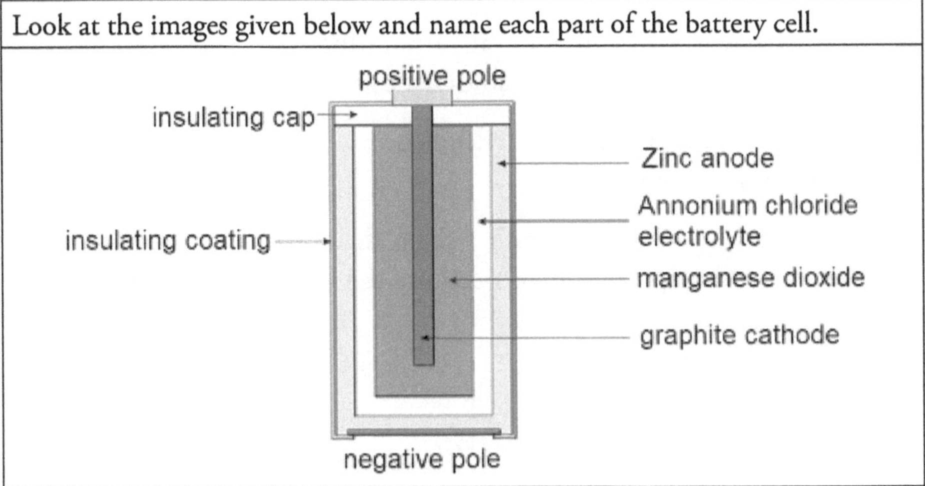

Use the materials given to you, assemble them and make a battery. Check whether it generates electricity or not.

Watch this video to learn how to assemble it in a better way.

https://www.youtube.com/watch?v=kbJPOsWlfN0

(For readers: I know from the text, you cannot copy it to watch the video. Therefore, I added a QR code below to scan it, so that you can see what is shown in the video.

Checklist:

1. Is the engagement idea aligned with the learning objective?

2. Is the engagement idea aligned with the lesson plan covering the relevant concept?

3. Is the engagement idea clear, concise, and easy for students to understand or use?

4. Is the engagement idea allowing the students to develop their understanding of the concept?

5. Is the engagement idea incorporating conceptual or real-life connection examples that students can easily relate to?

6. Is the engagement idea designed to be completed in a given timeframe of the session?

If you marked [Yes] for more than 5 from the above list, it simply means that the idea will help the students acquire the knowledge.

Plan #9	
Learning objective:	To engage in creating diverse electric circuits, exploring various circuit designs, components, and connections, and analysing their behaviours.
Taxonomy level:	Understanding
Summary of activity:	Begin the lesson by asking students what they know about the electric circuits and its types. Divide the students into small groups of 5 members each. Demonstrate how to make different types of circuits by explaining the differences between each. Give them the required materials and assign one type of circuit to each group. Use the materials to check whether it can have the flow of electricity. Summarise the topic with some more explanation.
Grouping configuration:	Group - they will be divided into small groups of 5 members each. They will be asked to make different types of electric circuits.
Teaching aids/ tools/ resources:	Battery, wires, bulbs

Checklist:

1. Is the planned activity aligned with the learning objective of the lesson?

2. Is the learning activity consisting of conceptual or real-life connections that will help the students understand its relevance and importance?

3. Is the learning activity working for small groups or as a whole-class activity or individually?

4. Is the learning activity providing opportunities for engaging in conceptual understanding?

5. Is the learning activity inclusive of opportunities for students to reflect on their learning and make connections to prior knowledge and experience?

6. Is the learning activity accommodating the different ability levels of the students in the classroom?

If you marked [Yes] for more than 5 from the above list, it simply means that the activity planned will work for the students.

Worksheet/ Engagement Idea #9:

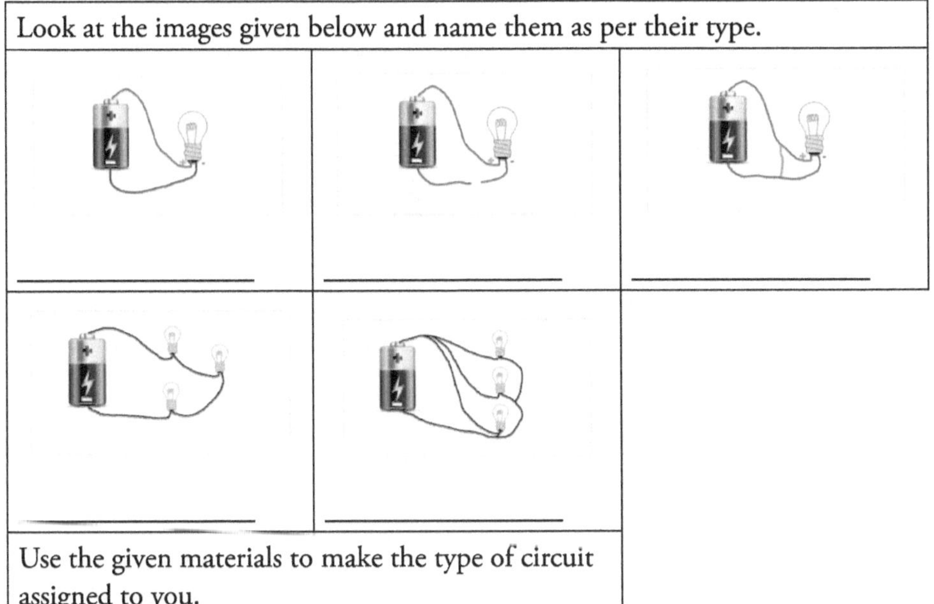

Look at the images given below and name them as per their type.

Use the given materials to make the type of circuit assigned to you.

Checklist:

1. Is the engagement idea aligned with the learning objective?

2. Is the engagement idea aligned with the lesson plan covering the relevant concept?

3. Is the engagement idea clear, concise, and easy for students to understand or use?

4. Is the engagement idea allowing the students to develop their understanding of the concept?

5. Is the engagement idea incorporating conceptual or real-life connection examples that students can easily relate to?

6. Is the engagement idea designed to be completed in a given timeframe of the session?

If you marked [Yes] for more than 5 from the above list, it simply means that the idea will help the students acquire the knowledge.

Plan #10	
Learning objective:	To construct various types of circuits, explore different configurations and components while analysing their effects on current flow, voltage, and resistance.
Taxonomy level:	Applying
Summary of activity:	Begin the lesson by asking students what they know about the electric circuits and its types.
	Divide the students into small groups of 5 members each. Show the diagrams of electric circuits and their types. Ask them to use the symbols of electric circuits and make diagrams as per the given instructions.
	Use the symbols to draw and demonstrate how to make short, parallel circuits, and series circuits.
	Summarise the topic with some more explanation.
Grouping configuration:	Individual – each student will be given a worksheet with symbols. They will be asked to make diagrams of the circuit as per the given instructions in the notebook.
Teaching aids/ tools/ resources:	Worksheet, circuit diagrams, symbols

Checklist:

1. Is the planned activity aligned with the learning objective of the lesson?

2. Is the learning activity consisting of conceptual or real-life connections that will help the students understand its relevance and importance?

3. Is the learning activity working for small groups or as a whole-class activity or individually?

4. Is the learning activity providing opportunities for engaging in conceptual understanding?

5. Is the learning activity inclusive of opportunities for students to reflect on their learning and make connections to prior knowledge and experience?

6. Is the learning activity accommodating the different ability levels of the students in the classroom?

If you marked [Yes] for more than 5 from the above list, it simply means that the activity planned will work for the students.

Worksheet/ Engagement Idea #10:

Use the symbols given below and make different circuits.	
Symbols	**Circuits to make**
	Closed circuit
	Open circuit
	Short circuit
	Series circuit
	Parallel circuit

Checklist:

1. Is the worksheet aligned with the learning objective?

2. Is the worksheet aligned with the lesson plan covering the relevant concept?

3. Is the worksheet clear, concise, and easy for students to understand or use?

4. Is the worksheet allowing the students to develop their understanding of the concept?

5. Is the worksheet incorporating conceptual or real-life connection examples that students can easily relate to?

6. Is the worksheet designed to be completed in a given timeframe of the session?

If you marked [Yes] for more than 5 from the above list, it simply means that the worksheet will help the students acquire the knowledge.

Plan #11	
Learning objective:	To analyse given circuits, identify and understand the components, connections, and flow of electricity, to effectively interpret circuit behaviour and make informed predictions about their functionality and potential outcomes.
Taxonomy level:	Analysis
Summary of activity:	Begin the lesson by asking students what they know about the electric circuits and its types. Divide the students into small groups of 5 members each. Give them incorrect diagrams of electric circuits. Ask them to discuss and analyse each incorrect circuit and explain what is wrong with it and how it should be corrected. Summarise the topic with some more explanation.
Grouping configuration:	Group – Students will be divided into groups. They will be asked to discuss and answer the questions.
Teaching aids/ tools/ resources:	Worksheet, incorrect circuit diagrams, symbols

Checklist:

1. Is the planned activity aligned with the learning objective of the lesson?

2. Is the learning activity consisting of conceptual or real-life connections that will help the students understand its relevance and importance?

3. Is the learning activity working for small groups or as a whole-class activity or individually?

4. Is the learning activity providing opportunities for engaging in conceptual understanding?

5. Is the learning activity inclusive of opportunities for students to reflect on their learning and make connections to prior knowledge and experience?

6. Is the learning activity accommodating the different ability levels of the students in the classroom?

If you marked more than 5 from the above list, it simply means that the activity planned will work for the students.

Worksheet/ Engagement Idea #11:

Look at the diagram below and analyse it.

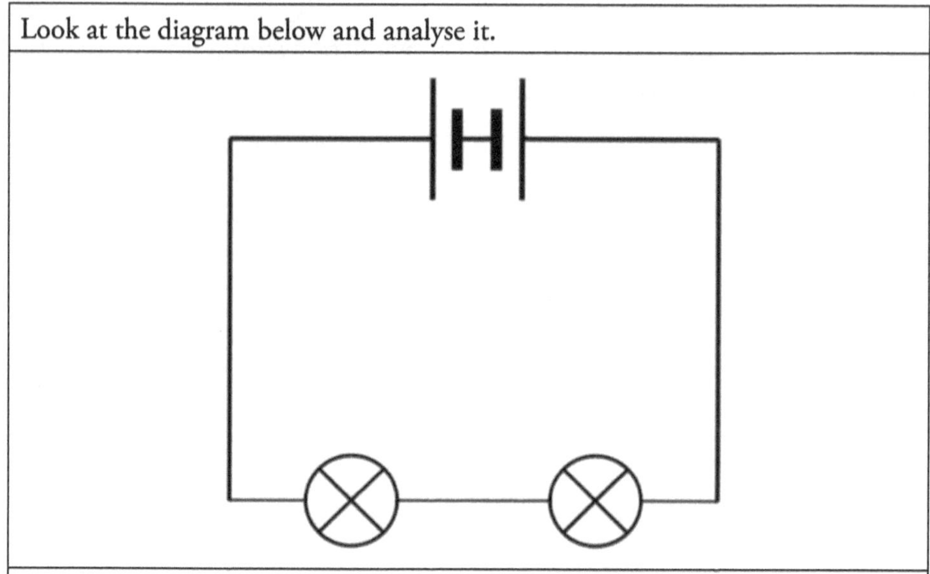

Look at each diagram and explain what is wrong with it and how it must be, to be right.

Checklist:

1. Is the worksheet aligned with the learning objective?

2. Is the worksheet aligned with the lesson plan covering the relevant concept?

3. Is the worksheet clear, concise, and easy for students to understand or use?

4. Is the worksheet allowing the students to develop their understanding of the concept?

5. Is the worksheet incorporating conceptual or real-life connection examples that students can easily relate to?

6. Is the worksheet designed to be completed in a given timeframe of the session?

If you marked [Yes] for more than 5 from the above list, it simply means that the worksheet will help the students acquire the knowledge.

Plan #12	
Learning objective:	To engage in the process of creating an electrical switch, gaining practical experience in circuitry, wiring, and electrical components, while exploring the significance and functionality of switches in controlling and regulating electrical circuits.
Taxonomy level:	Applying
Summary of activity:	Begin the lesson by asking students what they know about the electric switch. Divide the students into small groups of 5 members each. Give each group the required materials like wires, batteries, aluminium foil, bulbs, etc. Ask each group to use the materials to make a switch, connect it to a battery to check whether the electricity flows and light up the bulb. Summarise the topic with some more explanation.
Grouping configuration:	Group – Students will be divided into groups. They will be given materials to use and make a switch box.
Teaching aids/tools/resources:	Wires, battery cells, bulbs, aluminium foil, etc.

Checklist:

1. Is the planned activity aligned with the learning objective of the lesson?

2. Is the learning activity consisting of conceptual or real-life connections that will help the students understand its relevance and importance?

3. Is the learning activity working for small groups or as a whole-class activity or individually?

4. Is the learning activity providing opportunities for engaging in conceptual understanding?

5. Is the learning activity inclusive of opportunities for students to reflect on their learning and make connections to prior knowledge and experience?

6. Is the learning activity accommodating the different ability levels of the students in the classroom?

If you marked [Yes] for more than 5 from the above list, it simply means that the activity planned will work for the students.

Worksheet/ Engagement Idea #12:

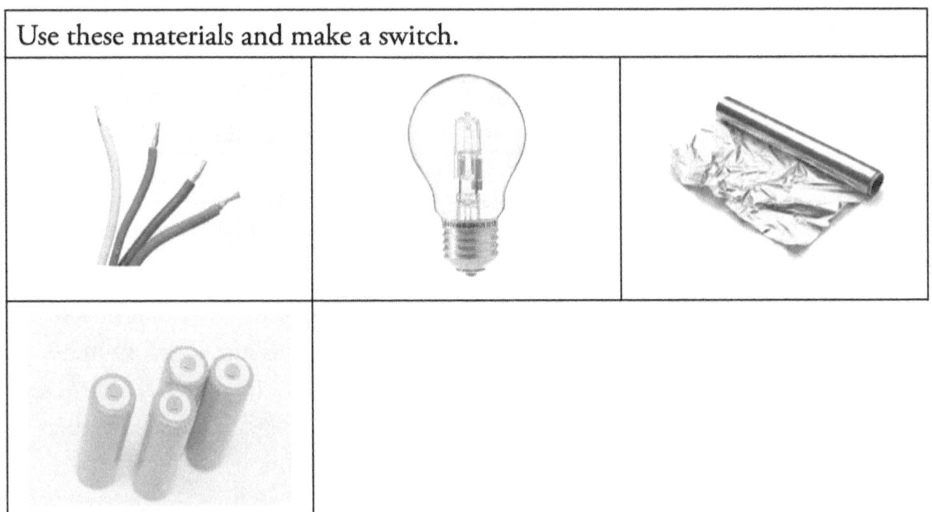

Checklist:

1. Is the engagement idea aligned with the learning objective?

2. Is the engagement idea aligned with the lesson plan covering the relevant concept?

3. Is the engagement idea clear, concise, and easy for students to understand or use?

4. Is the engagement idea allowing the students to develop their understanding of the concept?

5. Is the engagement idea incorporating conceptual or real-life connection examples that students can easily relate to?

6. Is the engagement idea designed to be completed in a given timeframe of the session?

If you marked [Yes] for more than 5 from the above list, it simply means that the idea will help the students acquire the knowledge.

Plan #13	
Learning objective:	To design and construct an electrical switch box, gaining hands-on experience in electrical circuitry, wiring, and safety protocols, while comprehending the importance and functionality of switches in controlling electrical flow.
Taxonomy level:	Applying
Summary of activity:	Begin the lesson by asking students what they know about the electric switch box. Divide the students into small groups of 5 members each. Give each group the required materials like wires, switches, indicators, etc. Ask each group to use the materials to make a switch box, and connect it to a battery to check whether the electricity flows. Summarise the topic with some more explanation.
Grouping configuration:	Group – Students will be divided into groups. They will be given materials to use and make a switchbox.
Teaching aids/ tools/ resources:	Switches, indicators, wires, battery, cutting player, screwdriver.

Checklist:

1. Is the planned activity aligned with the learning objective of the lesson?

2. Is the learning activity consisting of conceptual or real-life connections that will help the students understand its relevance and importance?

3. Is the learning activity working for small groups or as a whole-class activity or individually?

4. Is the learning activity providing opportunities for engaging in conceptual understanding?

5. Is the learning activity inclusive of opportunities for students to reflect on their learning and make connections to prior knowledge and experience?

6. Is the learning activity accommodating the different ability levels of the students in the classroom?

If you marked [Yes] for more than 5 from the above list, it simply means that the activity planned will work for the students.

Worksheet/ Engagement Idea #13:

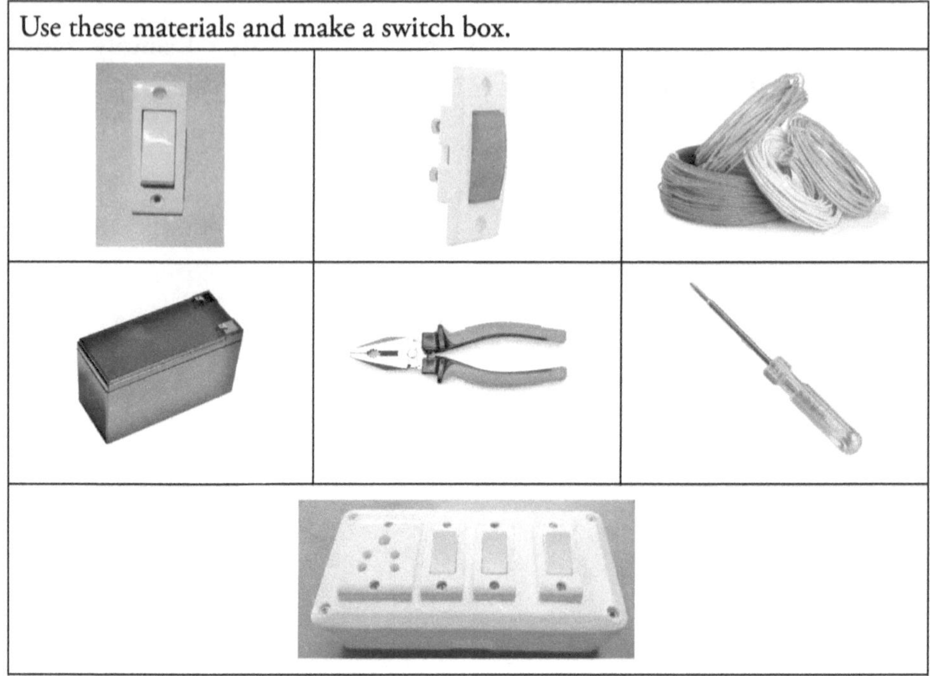

Checklist:

1. Is the engagement idea aligned with the learning objective?

2. Is the engagement idea aligned with the lesson plan covering the relevant concept?

3. Is the engagement idea clear, concise, and easy for students to understand or use?

4. Is the engagement idea allowing the students to develop their understanding of the concept?

5. Is the engagement idea incorporating conceptual or real-life connection examples that students can easily relate to?

6. Is the engagement idea designed to be completed in a given timeframe of the session?

If you marked [Yes] for more than 5 from the above list, it simply means that the idea will help the students acquire the knowledge.

Plan #14	
Learning objective:	To create various types of exhibits that demonstrate fundamental electrical concepts, showcasing their practical applications and promoting active exploration of electrical principles.
Taxonomy level:	Creating
Summary of activity:	Begin the lesson by asking students what they know about the different sources of energy.
	Divide the students into small groups of 5 members each. Give each group the required materials like wires, switches, indicators, and other tools/ materials required as per the type of project. Ask each group to use the materials to make an exhibit of the type of energy assigned. E.g. One group will make an exhibit of solar energy. One group will make an exhibit of nuclear power energy, likewise the other groups.
	Summarise the topic with some more explanation.
Grouping configuration:	Group – students will be divided into groups. They will be given materials to use and make the exhibits.
Teaching aids/ tools/ resources:	Switches, indicators, wires, battery, cutting player, screwdriver, battery cells, tapes,

Checklist:

1. Is the planned activity aligned with the learning objective of the lesson?

2. Is the learning activity consisting of conceptual or real-life connections that will help the students understand its relevance and importance?

3. Is the learning activity working for small groups or as a whole-class activity or individually?

4. Is the learning activity providing opportunities for engaging in conceptual understanding?

5. Is the learning activity inclusive of opportunities for students to reflect on their learning and make connections to prior knowledge and experience?

6. Is the learning activity accommodating the different ability levels of the students in the classroom?

If you marked more than 5 from the above list, it simply means that the activity planned will work for the students.

Worksheet/ Engagement Idea #14:

Use the given materials and make a model for the given source of energy.		
Nuclear Power Plant	Thermal Power Plant	Solar Power Plant
Hydroelectric Power Plant	Wind Power Plant	

**students will end the task by making similar models like the ones shown above

Checklist:

1. Is the engagement idea aligned with the learning objective?

2. Is the engagement idea aligned with the lesson plan covering the relevant concept?

3. Is the engagement idea clear, concise, and easy for students to understand or use?

4. Is the engagement idea allowing the students to develop their understanding of the concept?

5. Is the engagement idea incorporating conceptual or real-life connection examples that students can easily relate to?

6. Is the engagement idea designed to be completed in a given timeframe of the session?

If you marked [Yes] for more than 5 from the above list, it simply means that the idea will help the students acquire the knowledge.

Plan #15	
Learning objective:	To visit a power plant to observe and analyse the processes involved, understand the various components used, and explore the environmental and societal impacts of power generation and distribution.
Taxonomy level:	Understanding
Summary of activity:	Take students to two or more power plants. Ask them to observe the process of producing electricity. With the help of the expert from the power plant, explain the crucial points from each part of the process. Ask students to note down the points. Ask the students to submit a summary of the entire process of producing electricity.
Grouping configuration:	Whole class - to be taken to the power plant
Teaching aids/ tools/resources:	Summary Sheet

Checklist:

1. Is the planned activity aligned with the learning objective of the lesson?

2. Is the learning activity consisting of conceptual or real-life connections that will help the students understand its relevance and importance?

3. Is the learning activity working for small groups or as a whole-class activity or individually?

4. Is the learning activity providing opportunities for engaging in conceptual understanding?

5. Is the learning activity inclusive of opportunities for students to reflect on their learning and make connections to prior knowledge and experience?

6. Is the learning activity accommodating the different ability levels of the students in the classroom?

If you marked more than 5 from the above list, it simply means that the activity planned will work for the students.

Worksheet/Engagement Idea #15:

<table>
<tr><td colspan="3">Use the given sheet to summarise the process of producing electricity. You can pick any one power plant to summarise your learning.</td></tr>
<tr><td>Hydroelectric Power Plant</td><td>Thermal Power Plant</td><td>Solar Power Plant</td></tr>
</table>

3 things I learned today:

1. ....

   ....

2. ....

   ....

3. ....

   ....

2 things I found interesting:

1. ....

   ....

2. ....

   ....

1 thing I am still confused about:

1. ....

   ....

Checklist:

1. Is the worksheet aligned with the learning objective?

2. Is the worksheet aligned with the lesson plan covering the relevant concept?

3. Is the worksheet clear, concise, and easy for students to understand or use?

4. Is the Teworksheet allowing the students to develop their understanding of the concept?

5. Is the worksheet incorporating conceptual or real-life connection examples that students can easily relate to?

6. Is the worksheet designed to be completed in a given timeframe of the session?

If you marked [Yes] for more than 5 from the above list, it simply means that the worksheet will help the students acquire the knowledge.

Plan #16	
Learning objective:	To construct a functional generator, exploring its components and principles of operation to gain practical knowledge and understanding of electricity.
Taxonomy level:	Applying
Summary of activity:	Begin the lesson by asking students what they know about the electricity generator. Divide the students into small groups of 5 members each. Give each group the required materials and ask them to make a generator. Use the multimeter to check the electricity. Summarise the topic with some more explanation.
Grouping configuration:	Group – Students will be divided into groups. They will be given materials to use and make a generator.
Teaching aids/ tools/resources:	Coil, nails, cardboard sheets, nuts and bolts, LED lights, etc.

Checklist:

1. Is the planned activity aligned with the learning objective?

2. Is the planned activity aligned with the lesson plan covering the relevant concept?

3. Is the planned activity clear, concise, and easy for students to understand?

4. Is the planned activity allowing the students to develop their understanding of the concept?

5. Is the planned activity incorporating conceptual or real-life connection examples that students can easily relate to?

6. Is the planned activity designed to be completed in a given timeframe of the session?

If you marked more than 5 from the above list, it simply means that the activity planned will work for the students.

Worksheet/ Engagement Idea #16:

Use the given materials and make a model of a generator.

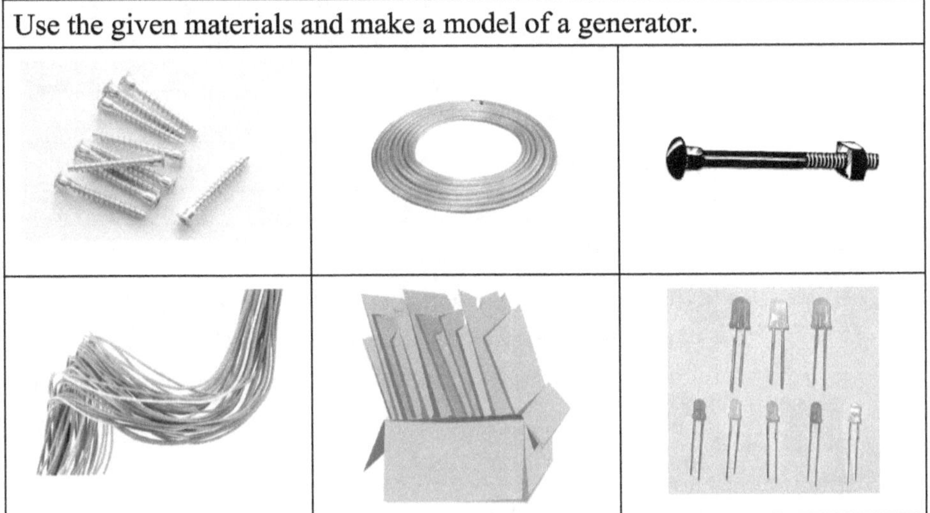

Checklist:

1. Is the engagement idea aligned with the learning objective?

2. Is the engagement idea aligned with the lesson plan covering the relevant concept?

3. Is the engagement idea clear, concise, and easy for students to understand or use?

4. Is the engagement idea allowing the students to develop their understanding of the concept?

5. Is the engagement idea incorporating conceptual or real-life connection examples that students can easily relate to?

6. Is the engagement idea designed to be completed in a given timeframe of the session?

If you marked [Yes] for more than 5 from the above list, it simply means that the idea will help the students acquire the knowledge.

Plan #17	
Learning objective:	To explore the characteristics, behaviours, and applications of static electricity and current electricity by identifying and comprehending the unique properties of each type of electrical phenomenon.
Taxonomy level:	Understanding
Summary of activity:	Begin the session by asking the students what they know about static electricity. Give each student a worksheet. Ask them to read the statements, and use the Venn diagram to classify the differences between static electricity and current electricity. Collect the worksheets. Summarise the concepts with some more clarification.
Grouping configuration:	Individuals - they will be given a worksheet to use and write the statements using the Venn diagram.
Teaching aids/ tools/ resources:	Worksheet, Venn diagram

Checklist:

1. Is the planned activity aligned with the learning objective of the lesson?

2. Is the learning activity consisting of conceptual or real-life connections that will help the students understand its relevance and importance?

3. Is the learning activity working for small groups or as a whole-class activity or individually?

4. Is the learning activity providing opportunities for engaging in conceptual understanding?

5. Is the learning activity inclusive of opportunities for students to reflect on their learning and make connections to prior knowledge and experience?

6. Is the learning activity accommodating the different ability levels of the students in the classroom?

If you marked [Yes] for more than 5 from the above list, it simply means that the activity planned will work for the students.

Worksheet/ Engagement Idea #17:

<table>
<tr><td>

Use a Venn diagram to classify the differences between static electricity and current electricity.

</td></tr>
<tr><td>

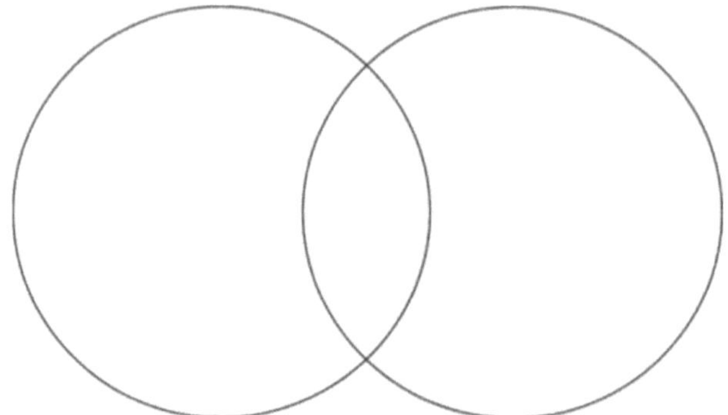

- a steady flow of electrons between object or places

- do not need a circuit.

- need to be powered by batteries or from a power plant (from outlets)

- charge builds up on the surface of an object.

</td></tr>
</table>

Checklist:

1. Is the worksheet aligned with the learning objective?

2. Is the worksheet aligned with the lesson plan covering the relevant concept?

3. Is the worksheet clear, concise, and easy for students to understand or use?

4. Is the worksheet allowing the students to develop their understanding of the concept?

5. Is the worksheet incorporating conceptual or real-life connection examples that students can easily relate to?

6. Is the worksheet designed to be completed in a given timeframe of the session?

If you marked [Yes] for more than 5 from the above list, it simply means that the worksheet will help the students acquire the knowledge.

Plan #18	
Learning objective:	To evaluate their understanding of electrical concepts by accurately determining whether given true or false statements about electricity are correct, demonstrating their grasp of key electrical principles and concepts.
Taxonomy level:	Evaluating
Summary of activity:	Begin the class by asking students some questions on electricity. Give each student a worksheet. Ask them to read the statements given and state whether they are true or false. Collect the worksheet and discuss the statements with the class. Summarise the concept with some more explanation.
Grouping configuration:	Individual – each student will be given a worksheet.
Teaching aids/ tools/ resources:	Worksheet

Checklist:

1. Is the planned activity aligned with the learning objective of the lesson?

2. Is the learning activity consisting of conceptual or real-life connections that will help the students understand its relevance and importance?

3. Is the learning activity working for small groups or as a whole-class activity or individually?

4. Is the learning activity providing opportunities for engaging in conceptual understanding?

5. Is the learning activity inclusive of opportunities for students to reflect on their learning and make connections to prior knowledge and experience?

6. Is the learning activity accommodating the different ability levels of the students in the classroom?

If you marked more than 5 from the above list, it simply means that the activity planned will work for the students.

Worksheet/ Engagement Idea #18:

<table>
<tr><td colspan="2">Read the statements given below. State True or False as per your understanding.</td></tr>
<tr><td>1. ________________</td><td>conductor allows the current to pass through it.</td></tr>
<tr><td>2. ________________</td><td>insulator doesn't allow the current to pass through it.</td></tr>
<tr><td>3. ________________</td><td>electric cell metal cap is a positive terminal.</td></tr>
<tr><td>4. ________________</td><td>electric cell disc is a negative terminal.</td></tr>
<tr><td>5. ________________</td><td>an electric cell has four terminals.</td></tr>
<tr><td>6. ________________</td><td>air is a good conductor of electricity.</td></tr>
</table>

Checklist:

1. Is the worksheet aligned with the learning objective?

2. Is the worksheet aligned with the lesson plan covering the relevant concept?

3. Is the worksheet clear, concise, and easy for students to understand or use?

4. Is the worksheet allowing the students to develop their understanding of the concept?

5. Is the worksheet incorporating conceptual or real-life connection examples that students can easily relate to?

6. Is the worksheet designed to be completed in a given timeframe of the session?

If you marked [Yes] for more than 5 from the above list, it simply means that the worksheet will help the students acquire the knowledge.

Plan #19	
Learning objective:	To demonstrate a comprehensive understanding of electricity concepts by explaining the principles of electrical circuits and their applications in real-world scenarios.
Taxonomy level:	Evaluating
Summary of activity:	Begin the session by asking the students about electricity concepts. Give each student a worksheet. Ask them to read the statements carefully and choose the most appropriate answer. Collect the worksheet and discuss the concepts further. Summarise the concept with more clarification on their responses.
Grouping configuration:	Individual – each student will be given a worksheet. They will be asked to read and complete it.
Teaching aids/ tools/ resources:	Worksheet

Checklist:

1. Is the planned activity aligned with the learning objective of the lesson?

2. Is the learning activity consisting of conceptual or real-life connections that will help the students understand its relevance and importance?

3. Is the learning activity working for small groups or as a whole-class activity or individually?

4. Is the learning activity providing opportunities for engaging in conceptual understanding?

5. Is the learning activity inclusive of opportunities for students to reflect on their learning and make connections to prior knowledge and experience?

6. Is the learning activity accommodating the different ability levels of the students in the classroom?

If you marked [Yes] for more than 5 from the above list, it simply means that the activity planned will work for the students.

Worksheet/ Engagement Idea #19:

Read the statements given below. Choose the most appropriate options for each statement.

1. Which of the following is a natural source of electricity?

   a) Lightning   b) Battery   c) Power plant   d) Solar panel

2. What unit is used to measure electrical resistance?

   a) Watts   b) Ohms   c) Volts   d) Amps

3. Which part of an atom carries an electric charge?

   a) Protons   b) Neutrons   c) Electrons   d) Nucleus

4. Which type of energy transformation occurs in a light bulb when it produces light?

   a) Electrical to mechanical   b) Electrical to thermal

   c) Electrical to light   d) Electrical to sound

5. What is the rate at which electric energy is converted into other forms of energy called?

   a) Current   b) Voltage   c) Power   d) Resistance

6. What is the path that electricity takes through a circuit called?

   a) Line   b) Route   c) Circuit   d) Trail

Checklist:

1. Is the worksheet aligned with the learning objective?

2. Is the worksheet aligned with the lesson plan covering the relevant concept?

3. Is the worksheet clear, concise, and easy for students to understand or use?

4. Is the worksheet allowing the students to develop their understanding of the concept?

5. Is the worksheet incorporating conceptual or real-life connection examples that students can easily relate to?

6. Is the worksheet designed to be completed in a given timeframe of the session?

If you marked [Yes] for more than 5 from the above list, it simply means that the worksheet will help the students acquire the knowledge.

Plan #20	
Learning objective:	To conduct a case study on different sources of energy used for producing electricity by analysing and evaluating various energy sources, exploring their advantages, disadvantages, environmental impacts, and technological applications.
Taxonomy level:	Evaluating
Summary of activity:	Begin the session by asking students what they know about different sources of electricity. Divide the students into small groups of 5 members each. Give each group one type of energy to read, research and do a case study. Explain the aspects to keep in mind while doing it and show the format. Collect the case study and summarise the topic with some more clarification.
Grouping configuration:	Group - they will be divided into small groups of 5 members each. They will be asked to make a case study of the source of energy assigned.
Teaching aids/ tools/ resources:	Worksheet, Templates

Checklist:

1. Is the planned activity aligned with the learning objective of the lesson?

2. Is the learning activity consisting of conceptual or real-life connections that will help the students understand its relevance and importance?

3. Is the learning activity working for small groups or as a whole-class activity or individually?

4. Is the learning activity providing opportunities for engaging in conceptual understanding?

5. Is the learning activity inclusive of opportunities for students to reflect on their learning and make connections to prior knowledge and experience?

6. Is the learning activity accommodating the different ability levels of the students in the classroom?

If you marked [Yes] for more than 5 from the above list, it simply means that the activity planned will work for the students.

Worksheet/ Engagement Idea #20:

Use the template to make your case study.

1. Title:
   - Give a relevant title to the case study.
2. Introduction:
   - Provide an overview of the case study's purpose and objectives.
   - Introduce the source of energy that will be analysed in the case study.
3. Methodology:
   - Describe the criteria used to select the energy sources for analysis.
4. Case Study Analysis:
   - A. Energy Source 1: Write the source of energy you are working on.
     - Describe the energy source chosen for the case study.
     - Analyse its characteristics, including availability, abundance, challenges, and environmental impact.
     - Present real-world examples of its applications and success stories.
   - B. Evaluation:
     - Evaluate the suitability of each energy source for different regions and specific energy needs.
5. Case Study Findings:
   - Summarise the key findings from the case study analysis.
   - Identify any trends and patterns
6. Conclusion:
   - Recap the main points discussed in the case study.
7. Recommendations:
   - Offer recommendations for policymakers, stakeholders, and individuals on sustainable energy choices and future developments in the energy sector.
8. References:
   - List all the sources cited throughout the case study.
9. Appendices:
   - Include any additional information or data that supports the case study analysis (e.g., charts, graphs, images).

Checklist:

1. Is the engagement idea aligned with the learning objective?

2. Is the engagement idea aligned with the lesson plan covering the relevant concept?

3. Is the engagement idea clear, concise, and easy for students to understand or use?

4. Is the engagement idea allowing the students to develop their understanding of the concept?

5. Is the engagement idea incorporating conceptual or real-life connection examples that students can easily relate to?

6. Is the engagement designed to be completed in a given timeframe of the session?

If you marked [Yes] for more than 5 from the above list, it simply means that the idea will help the students acquire the knowledge.

Plan #21	
Learning objective:	To examine each component of different sources of energy used for producing electricity and identify their respective functions in the electricity generation process.
Taxonomy level:	Understanding
Summary of activity:	Begin the session by asking the students what they know about the different parts of a wind power plant. Show each student a picture of different power plants, ask them to name the parts of each and describe in detail its function. Summarise the concepts with some more clarification.
Grouping configuration:	Group - students will be divided into small groups of 5 members each. They will be given a picture to look at, examine and describe the parts and their functions in generating electricity.
Teaching aids/ tools/resources:	Pictures

Checklist:

1. Is the planned activity aligned with the learning objective of the lesson?

2. Is the learning activity consisting of conceptual or real-life connections that will help the students understand its relevance and importance?

3. Is the learning activity working for small groups or as a whole-class activity or individually?

4. Is the learning activity providing opportunities for engaging in conceptual understanding?

5. Is the learning activity inclusive of opportunities for students to reflect on their learning and make connections to prior knowledge and experience?

6. Is the learning activity accommodating the different ability levels of the students in the classroom?

If you marked [Yes] for more than 5 from the above list, it simply means that the activity planned will work for the students.

Worksheet/ Engagement Idea #21:

Look at the components of each source of energy given. Look and describe
their functions.

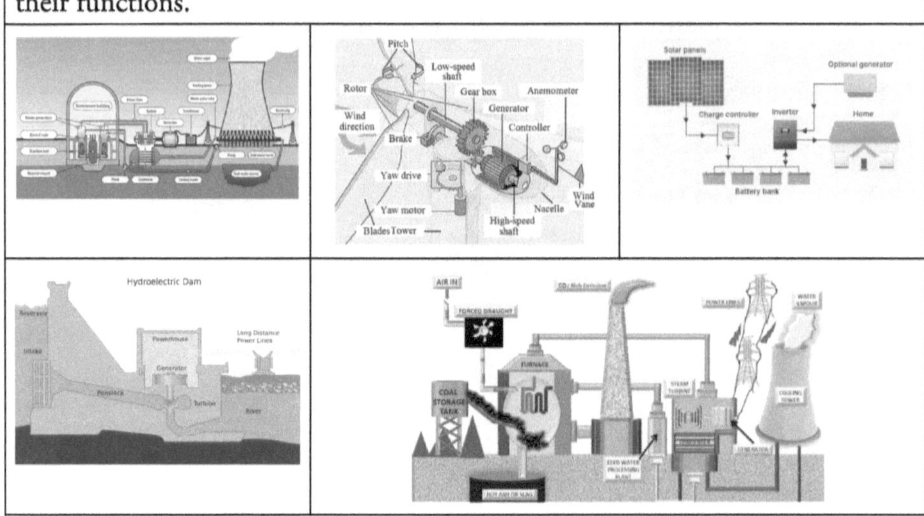

Checklist:

1. Is the engagement idea aligned with the learning objective?

2. Is the engagement idea aligned with the lesson plan covering the relevant concept?

3. Is the engagement idea clear, concise, and easy for students to understand or use?

4. Is the engagement idea allowing the students to develop their understanding of the concept?

5. Is the engagement idea incorporating conceptual or real-life connection examples that students can easily relate to?

6. Is the engagement idea designed to be completed in a given timeframe of the session?

If you marked [Yes] for more than 5 from the above list, it simply means
that the idea will help the students acquire the knowledge.

Plan #22	
Learning objective:	To visually observe the key steps and components involved in producing and delivering electricity, enhancing their knowledge of the energy generation and supply chain.
Taxonomy level:	Understanding
Summary of activity:	Begin the session by asking the students what they know about electricity supply and how it's produced. Play a video that explains the process of generating electricity with one or two sources of energy, how it is stored, and how it is supplied to the communities and commercial areas. Summarise the concept with some more clarification.
Grouping configuration:	Whole class - to watch a video and note the key aspects of producing electricity and supplying it.
Teaching aids/ tools/resources:	Video

Checklist:

1. Is the planned activity aligned with the learning objective of the lesson?

2. Is the learning activity consisting of conceptual or real-life connections that will help the students understand its relevance and importance?

3. Is the learning activity working for small groups or as a whole-class activity or individually?

4. Is the learning activity providing opportunities for engaging in conceptual understanding?

5. Is the learning activity inclusive of opportunities for students to reflect on their learning and make connections to prior knowledge and experience?

6. Is the learning activity accommodating the different ability levels of the students in the classroom?

If you marked [Yes] for more than 5 from the above list, it simply means that the activity planned will work for the students.

Worksheet/ Engagement Idea #22:

Watch this video and note down the key aspects.	
Video link:	https://www.youtube.com/watch?v=e6IpOcztJ50
QR Code of the video:	

Checklist:

1. Is the engagement idea aligned with the learning objective?

2. Is the engagement idea aligned with the lesson plan covering the relevant concept?

3. Is the engagement idea clear, concise, and easy for students to understand or use?

4. Is the engagement idea allowing the students to develop their understanding of the concept?

5. Is the engagement idea incorporating conceptual or real-life connection examples that students can easily relate to?

6. Is the engagement idea designed to be completed in a given timeframe of the session?

If you marked [Yes] for more than 5 from the above list, it simply means that the idea will help the students acquire the knowledge.

Plan #23	
Learning objective:	To actively reinforce their understanding of electrical terminology, connections between different concepts, and practical applications.
Taxonomy level:	Remembering
Summary of activity:	Begin the lesson by asking students what they know about the uses of electricity. Give each student a worksheet puzzle to solve. Ask them to read the clues carefully and solve them. Collect the worksheets and ask each student to tell the terminologies they learned or recalled with the activity.
Grouping configuration:	Individual – each student will be given a worksheet puzzle to solve.
Teaching aids/ tools/resources:	Crossword puzzle

Checklist:

1. Is the planned activity aligned with the learning objective of the lesson?

2. Is the learning activity consisting of conceptual or real-life connections that will help the students understand its relevance and importance?

3. Is the learning activity working for small groups or as a whole-class activity or individually?

4. Is the learning activity providing opportunities for engaging in conceptual understanding?

5. Is the learning activity inclusive of opportunities for students to reflect on their learning and make connections to prior knowledge and experience?

6. Is the learning activity accommodating the different ability levels of the students in the classroom?

If you marked [Yes] for more than 5 from the above list, it simply means that the activity planned will work for the students.

Worksheet/ Engagement Idea #23:

Read the clues carefully and solve the puzzle.

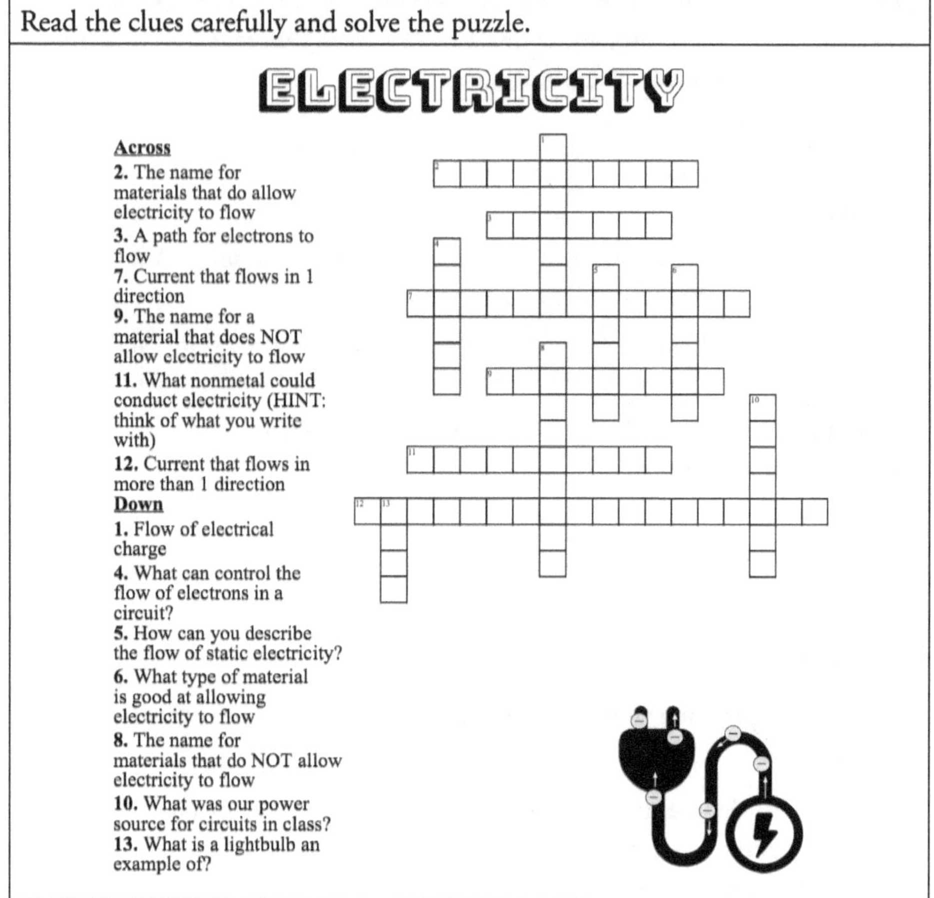

Checklist:

1. Is the worksheet activity aligned with the learning objective?

2. Is the worksheet activity aligned with the lesson plan covering the relevant concept?

3. Is the worksheet activity clear, concise, and easy for students to understand or use?

4. Is the worksheet activity allowing the students to develop their understanding of the concept?

5. Is the worksheet activity incorporating conceptual or real-life connection examples that students can easily relate to?

6. Is the worksheet activity designed to be completed in a given timeframe of the session?

If you marked [Yes] for more than 5 from the above list, it simply means that the worksheet will help the students acquire the knowledge.

Plan #24	
Learning objective:	To confidently lead their fellow classmates in an educational presentation about electricity, demonstrating a thorough understanding of key concepts, safety measures, and techniques.
Taxonomy level:	Applying
Summary of activity:	Begin the lesson by asking students what they have prepared to present to their classmates. Ask each student to come forward. Give 5 minutes to each student to present the source of energy he/she has worked on for the presentation and lead the session. Ask other students to note down the points and clarify their doubts in the end. Do this with 5 or 6 students. Summarise the concept with some more clarification.
Grouping configuration:	Individual – some students will be given an opportunity to lead the session.
Teaching aids/ tools/resources:	

**students will be informed in advance about leading the session, so they go home and come prepared the next day.

Checklist:

1. Is the planned activity aligned with the learning objective of the lesson?

2. Is the learning activity consisting of conceptual or real-life connections that will help the students understand its relevance and importance?

3. Is the learning activity working for small groups or as a whole-class activity or individually?

4. Is the learning activity providing opportunities for engaging in conceptual understanding?

5. Is the learning activity inclusive of opportunities for students to reflect on their learning and make connections to prior knowledge and experience?

6. Is the learning activity accommodating the different ability levels of the students in the classroom?

If you marked [Yes] for more than 5 from the above list, it simply means that the activity planned will work for the students.

Worksheet/ Engagement Idea #24:

Use the given points to present the source of energy that you have worked on for the presentation:		
Hydroelectric Power Plant	Thermal Power Plant	Solar Power Plant

5 things to know about this source of energy:

1. ....

....

2. ....

....

3. ....

....

4. ....

....

5. ....

....

3 things to remember about this energy:

1. ....

....

2. ....

....

3. ....

....

2 things to think over about its sustainability:

1. ....

....

2. ....

....

Checklist:

1. Is the worksheet aligned with the learning objective?

2. Is the worksheet aligned with the lesson plan covering the relevant concept?

3. Is the worksheet clear, concise, and easy for students to understand?

4. Is the worksheet allowing the students to develop their understanding of the concept?

5. Is the worksheet incorporating conceptual or real-life connection examples that students can easily relate to?

6. Is the worksheet designed to be completed in a given timeframe of the session?

If you marked [Yes] for more than 5 from the above list, it simply means that the worksheet will help the students acquire the knowledge.

Plan #25	
Learning objective:	To create a comprehensive mind map that visually organises and categorises various sources of energy, including their characteristics, advantages, and disadvantages, thereby demonstrating a deeper understanding of the diverse sources of energy used in electricity generation.
Taxonomy level:	Applying
Summary of activity:	Begin the lesson by asking students what they know about the different sources of energy. Make groups of students, and ask them to brainstorm as many different purposes of electricity as they can think of. Assign one source of energy to each group. Ask each group to make a mind map of the source of energy assigned by mentioning its characteristics, advantages, limitations, and new techniques to generate electricity using the source. Give each student a worksheet and summarise the concept.
Grouping configuration:	Group - students will be divided into small groups to discuss the different sources of electricity with peers and complete the given task.
Teaching aids/ tools/ resources:	Worksheet, Mind map

Checklist:

1. Is the planned activity aligned with the learning objective of the lesson?

2. Is the learning activity consisting of conceptual or real-life connections that will help the students understand its relevance and importance?

3. Is the learning activity working for small groups or as a whole-class activity or individually?

4. Is the learning activity providing opportunities for engaging in conceptual understanding?

5. Is the learning activity inclusive of opportunities for students to reflect on their learning and make connections to prior knowledge and experience?

6. Is the learning activity accommodating the different ability levels of the students in the classroom?

If you marked [Yes] for more than 5 from the above list, it simply means that the activity planned will work for the students.

Worksheet/ Engagement Idea #25:

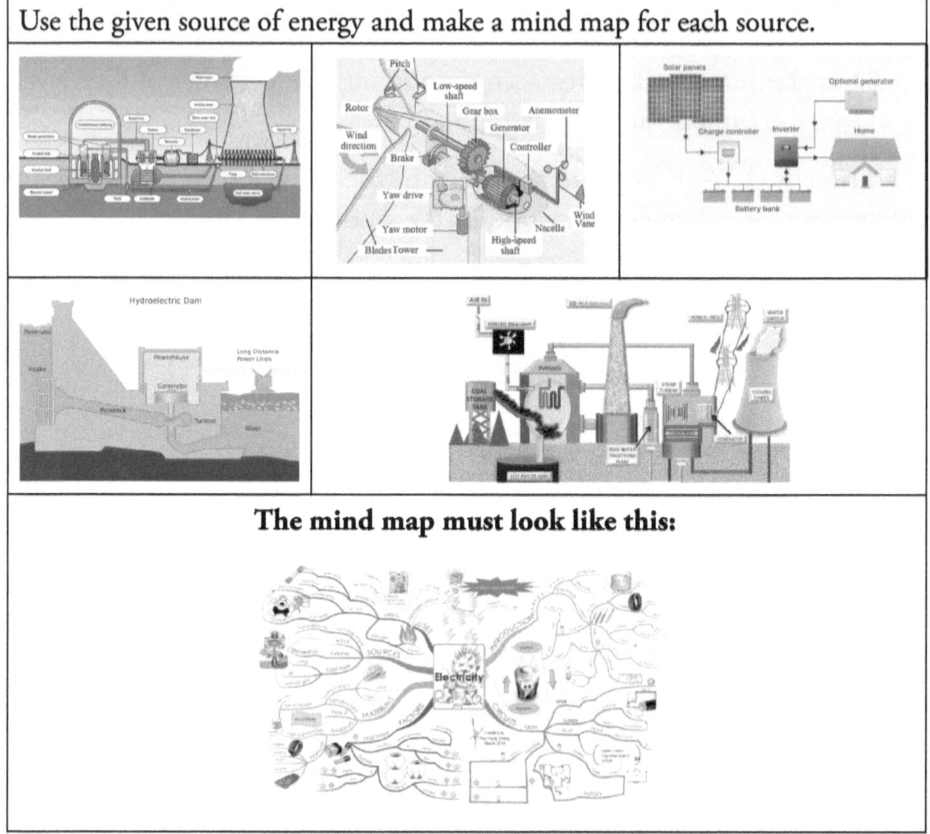

Checklist:

1. Is the worksheet aligned with the learning objective?

2. Is the worksheet aligned with the lesson plan covering the relevant concept?

3. Is the worksheet clear, concise, and easy for students to understand or use?

4. Is the worksheet allowing the students to develop their understanding of the concept?

5. Is the worksheet incorporating conceptual or real-life connection examples that students can easily relate to?

6. Is the worksheet designed to be completed in a given timeframe of the session?

If you marked [Yes] for more than 5 from the above list, it simply means that the worksheet will help the students acquire the knowledge.

List of plans explained:

S. no.	Plans	Bloom's Taxonomy levels incorporated
	To accurately recall and articulate......	Level 1
	To define and articulate......	Level 1
	To identify conducive and non-conducive......	Level 1
	To accurately label and differentiate......	Level 1
	To define and describe the source of energy......	Level 1
	To compare and contrast two or three......	Level 2
	To identify and differentiate components......	Level 2
	To understand the functioning of electric cells......	Level 2
	To engage in creating diverse electric......	Level 2
	To construct various types of circuits......	Level 3
	To analyse the given circuit......	Level 4
	To engage in the process of creating an electrical......	Level 3
	To design and construct an electrical......	Level 3
	To create various types of exhibits......	Level 6
	To visit the power plant......	Level 2
	To construct a functional generator......	Level 2
	To explore the characteristics, behaviours, ...	Level 2
	To evaluate their understanding of electrical......	Level 5
	To demonstrate a comprehensive understanding......	Level 5
	To conduct a case study......	Level 5
	To examine each component of	Level 2
	To visually observe the key components......	Level 2
	To actively reinforce their understanding......	Level 1
	To confidently lead their fellow students......	Level 3
	To create a mind map that visually......	Level 3

Lesson #2 "Shapes and Angles"

Subject: Mathematics

This lesson has been taken from Grade 5 NCERT Textbook.

Scan this QR Code to read content of the lesson.

Plan #1	
Learning objective:	To accurately recall and describe various shapes and angles by utilising flashcards as a study aid.
Taxonomy level:	Remembering
Summary of activity:	Begin the lesson by asking students what they know about the shapes and angles. Make groups of students, and give each group a set of flashcards with shapes and angles (one side a shape or an angle, the other side the description). Ask them to look at the shapes and angles, read the description and describe what they know about each. Summarise the key concepts with some more clarification.
Grouping configuration:	Group - students will be divided into small groups to use the flashcards and discuss and describe the shapes and angles in their own words.
Teaching aids/ tools/ resources:	Flashcards

Checklist:

1. Is the planned activity aligned with the learning objective of the lesson?

2. Is the learning activity consisting of conceptual or real-life connections that will help the students understand its relevance and importance?

3. Is the learning activity working for small groups or as a whole-class activity or individually?

4. Is the learning activity providing opportunities for engaging in conceptual understanding?

5. Is the learning activity inclusive of opportunities for students to reflect on their learning and make connections to prior knowledge and experience?

6. Is the learning activity accommodating the different ability levels of the students in the classroom?

If you marked [Yes] for more than 5 from the above list, it simply means that the activity planned will work for the students.

Worksheet/ Engagement Idea #2:

<table>
<tr><td colspan="2">Look at the flashcards given below, read the description given at the back and describe what you understand by these shapes and angles.</td></tr>
<tr><td></td><td></td></tr>
<tr><td>an angle measuring less than 90 degrees</td><td>an angle measuring 90 degrees</td></tr>
<tr><td></td><td></td></tr>
</table>

Checklist:

1. Is the learning material aligned with the learning objective?

2. Is the learning material aligned with the lesson plan covering the relevant concept?

3. Is the learning material clear, concise, and easy for students to understand or use?

4. Is the learning material allowing the students to develop their understanding of the concept?

5. Is the learning material incorporating conceptual or real-life connection examples that students can easily relate to?

6. Is the learning material designed to be completed in a given timeframe of the session?

If you marked [Yes] for more than 5 from the above list, it simply means that the idea will help the students acquire the knowledge.

Plan #2	
Learning objective:	To demonstrate proficiency in identifying and matching various shapes and angles by correctly associating them with their corresponding options.
Taxonomy level:	Remembering
Summary of activity:	Begin the lesson by asking students what they know about the shapes and angles. Give each student a worksheet. Ask each student to read the statement given and match them to the appropriate shapes and angles given in the second column. Summarise the concept with some more explanation/clarification.
Grouping configuration:	Individual – each student will be given a worksheet. They will be asked to read and do the worksheet.
Teaching aids/ tools/resources:	Worksheet, Pictures of shapes and angles.

Checklist:

1. Is the planned activity aligned with the learning objective of the lesson?

2. Is the learning activity consisting of conceptual or real-life connections that will help the students understand its relevance and importance?

3. Is the learning activity working for small groups or as a whole-class activity or individually?

4. Is the learning activity providing opportunities for engaging in conceptual understanding?

5. Is the learning activity inclusive of opportunities for students to reflect on their learning and make connections to prior knowledge and experience?

6. Is the learning activity accommodating the different ability levels of the students in the classroom?

If you marked [Yes] for more than 5 from the above list, it simply means that the activity planned will work for the students.

Worksheet/ Engagement Idea #2:

Read the description given below and match them to their actual shape or angle.	
1. A parallelogram with all right angles and two pairs of parallel sides	
2. A parallelogram with all sides the same length	
3. A parallelogram with all sides the same length and all right angles	
4. An angle measuring more than 90 degrees	
5. An angle measuring less than 90 degrees	

Checklist:

1. Is the worksheet aligned with the learning objective?

2. Is the worksheet aligned with the lesson plan covering the relevant concept?

3. Is the worksheet clear, concise, and easy for students to understand or use?

4. Is the worksheet allowing the students to develop their understanding of the concept?

5. Is the worksheet incorporating conceptual or real-life connection examples that students can easily relate to?

6. Is the worksheet designed to be completed in a given timeframe of the session?

If you marked [Yes] for more than 5 from the above list, it simply means that the worksheet will help the students acquire the knowledge.

Plan #3	
Learning objective:	To proficiently construct various shapes and angles using the provided materials, thereby gaining a comprehensive understanding of shapes and angles.
Taxonomy level:	Understanding
Summary of activity:	Begin the lesson by asking students what they know about the shapes and angles.
	Divide the students into small groups. Give each group some materials like straws, popsicle sticks, matchsticks, etc., and ask them to use the materials and make the shapes and angles as per the given instructions.
	Summarise the concept with some more explanation/clarification.
Grouping configuration:	Group – students to be divided into small groups. Each group will be instructed to make the shapes and angles by using the given materials.
Teaching aids/ tools/ resources:	Clay, popsicle sticks, matchsticks, straws.

Checklist:

1. Is the planned activity aligned with the learning objective of the lesson?

2. Is the learning activity consisting of conceptual or real-life connections that will help the students understand its relevance and importance?

3. Is the learning activity working for small groups or as a whole-class activity or individually?

4. Is the learning activity providing opportunities for engaging in conceptual understanding?

5. Is the learning activity inclusive of opportunities for students to reflect on their learning and make connections to prior knowledge and experience?

6. Is the learning activity accommodating the different ability levels of the students in the classroom?

If you marked [Yes] for more than 5 from the above list, it simply means that the activity planned will work for the students.

Worksheet/ Engagement Idea #3:

<table>
<tr><td>

Use the given materials and make the shapes and angles as per the given instructions:

Example:

- *Group one: Make an acute angle*
- *Group two: Make a rhombus/ rectangle*

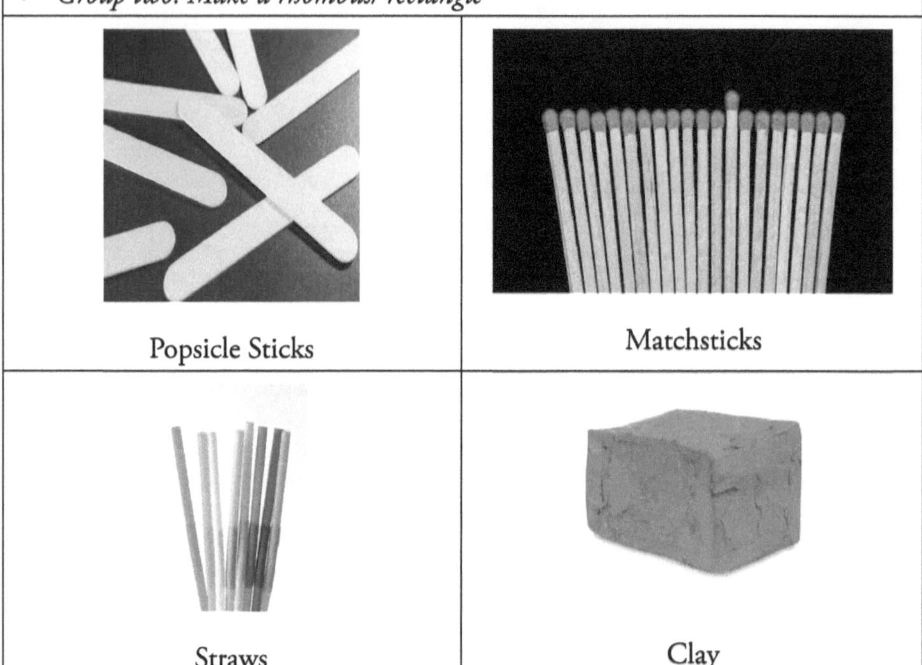

Popsicle Sticks	Matchsticks
Straws	Clay

</td></tr>
</table>

Checklist:

1. Is the learning material aligned with the learning objective?

2. Is the learning material aligned with the lesson plan covering the relevant concept?

3. Is the learning material clear, concise, and easy for students to understand or use?

4. Is the learning material allowing the students to develop their understanding of the concept?

5. Is the learning material incorporating conceptual or real-life connection examples that students can easily relate to?

6. Is the learning material designed to be completed in a given timeframe of the session?

If you marked [Yes] for more than 5 from the above list, it simply means that the idea will help the students acquire the knowledge.

Plan #4	
Learning objective:	To identify different shapes and angles present within the classroom or school environment, thereby developing a practical understanding of shapes and angles in real-world contexts.
Taxonomy level:	Understanding
Summary of activity:	Begin the lesson by asking students what they know about the shapes and angles. Divide the students into small groups. Ask each group to go to a corner of the classroom or any area chosen for the group outside the classroom. Ask them to look at the things they see over there and identify the shapes and angles in them. Ask them to come back to the class and share what they found. Summarise the concept with some more explanation/ clarification.
Grouping configuration:	Group – students are to be divided into small groups. Each group will be asked to visit a particular corner of the class or outside the class to find the shapes and angles.
Teaching aids/ tools/ resources:	List of things they identified

Checklist:

1. Is the planned activity aligned with the learning objective of the lesson?

2. Is the learning activity consisting of conceptual or real-life connections that will help the students understand its relevance and importance?

3. Is the learning activity working for small groups or as a whole-class activity or individually?

4. Is the learning activity providing opportunities for engaging in conceptual understanding?

5. Is the learning activity inclusive of opportunities for students to reflect on their learning and make connections to prior knowledge and experience?

6. Is the learning activity accommodating the different ability levels of the students in the classroom?

If you marked [Yes] for more than 5 from the above list, it simply means that the activity planned will work for the students.

Worksheet/ Engagement Idea #4:

Use the given sheet to write the things you looked at and the number of shapes and angles you identified.		
What things did you look at during your observation?	No. of shapes you identified	No. of angles you identified

Checklist:

1. Is the worksheet aligned with the learning objective?

2. Is the worksheet aligned with the lesson plan covering the relevant concept?

3. Is the worksheet clear, concise, and easy for students to understand or use?

4. Is the worksheet allowing the students to develop their understanding of the concept?

5. Is the worksheet incorporating conceptual or real-life connection examples that students can easily relate to?

6. Is the worksheet designed to be completed in a given timeframe of the session?

If you marked [Yes] for more than 5 from the above list, it simply means that the worksheet will help the students acquire the knowledge.

Plan #5	
Learning objective:	To accurately transform the given shapes and angles into their desired forms, follow the provided instructions.
Taxonomy level:	Analysing
Summary of activity:	Begin the lesson by asking students what they know about the shapes and angles. Divide the students into small groups. Give each group some shapes and angles that are made of different materials. Ask each group to look at them and transform them into the desired forms of shapes and angles as per the instructions. Summarise the concept with some more explanation/ clarification.
Grouping configuration:	Group – students will be divided into small groups. Each group will be asked to take the models of shapes and angles, and then transform them into other forms.
Teaching aids/ tools/ resources:	Matchsticks

Checklist:

1. Is the planned activity aligned with the learning objective of the lesson?

2. Is the learning activity consisting of conceptual or real-life connections that will help the students understand its relevance and importance?

3. Is the learning activity working for small groups or as a whole-class activity or individually?

4. Is the learning activity providing opportunities for engaging in conceptual understanding?

5. Is the learning activity inclusive of opportunities for students to reflect on their learning and make connections to prior knowledge and experience?

6. Is the learning activity accommodating the different ability levels of the students in the classroom?

If you marked [Yes] for more than 5 from the above list, it simply means that the activity planned will work for the students.

Worksheet/ Engagement Idea #5:

Change these shapes into other shapes as per the instructions.	
Change it into a rectangle	Change it into an obtuse angle
Change it into a pentagon	Change it into a hexagon
Change it into an acute angle	Change it into a square

Checklist:

1. Is the learning material aligned with the learning objective?

2. Is the learning material aligned with the lesson plan covering the relevant concept?

3. Is the learning material clear, concise, and easy for students to understand or use?

4. Is the learning material allowing the students to develop their understanding of the concept?

5. Is the learning material incorporating conceptual or real-life connection examples that students can easily relate to?

6. Is the learning material designed to be completed in a given timeframe of the session?

If you marked [Yes] for more than 5 from the above list, it simply means that the idea will help the students acquire the knowledge.

Plan #6	
Learning objective:	To identify shapes and angles with a comprehensive understanding of shapes and angles in practical visual contexts.
Taxonomy level:	Understanding
Summary of activity:	Begin the lesson by asking students what they know about the shapes and angles. Give each student a worksheet with a picture on it. Ask each student to look at the picture and identify the shapes and angles in it. Ask them to write the number of shapes and angles they identified in the box given below. Summarise the concept with some more explanation/ clarification.
Grouping configuration:	Individual – students will be asked to look at the picture and do the worksheet.
Teaching aids/ tools/ resources:	Worksheet, Pictures

Checklist:

1. Is the planned activity aligned with the learning objective of the lesson?

2. Is the learning activity consisting of conceptual or real-life connections that will help the students understand its relevance and importance?

3. Is the learning activity working for small groups or as a whole-class activity or individually?

4. Is the learning activity providing opportunities for engaging in conceptual understanding?

5. Is the learning activity inclusive of opportunities for students to reflect on their learning and make connections to prior knowledge and experience?

6. Is the learning activity accommodating the different ability levels of the students in the classroom?

If you marked [Yes] for more than 5 from the above list, it simply means that the activity planned will work for the students.

Worksheet/Engagement Idea #6:

Use the given sheet to write the things you looked at and the number of shapes and angles you identified.

No. of shapes identified	**No. of angles identified**
•	• ....
•	• ....
•	• ....

Checklist:

1. Is the worksheet aligned with the learning objective?

2. Is the worksheet aligned with the lesson plan covering the relevant concept?

3. Is the worksheet clear, concise, and easy for students to understand or use?

4. Is the worksheet allowing the students to develop their understanding of the concept?

5. Is the worksheet incorporating conceptual or real-life connection examples that students can easily relate to?

6. Is the worksheet designed to be completed in a given timeframe of the session?

If you marked [Yes] for more than 5 from the above list, it simply means that the worksheet will help the students acquire the knowledge.

Plan #7	
Learning objective:	To develop a solid understanding of shapes, angles, and spatial relationships, enhancing their problem-solving and geometric reasoning skills.
Taxonomy level:	Applying
Summary of activity:	Begin the lesson by asking students what they know about the shapes and angles. Divide the students into small groups. Give each group the tangram blocks. Assign each group four or five shapes of animals to make using the blocks. Summarise the concept with some more explanation/clarification.
Grouping configuration:	Group – students are to be divided into small groups. They can be asked to make shapes of animals using tangram blocks.
Teaching aids/ tools/resources:	Tangram blocks

Checklist:

1. Is the planned activity aligned with the learning objective of the lesson?

2. Is the learning activity consisting of conceptual or real-life connections that will help the students understand its relevance and importance?

3. Is the learning activity working for small groups or as a whole-class activity or individually?

4. Is the learning activity providing opportunities for engaging in conceptual understanding?

5. Is the learning activity inclusive of opportunities for students to reflect on their learning and make connections to prior knowledge and experience?

6. Is the learning activity accommodating the different ability levels of the students in the classroom?

If you marked [Yes] for more than 5 from the above list, it simply means that the activity planned will work for the students.

Worksheet/ Engagement Idea #7:

Use the tangram blocks to make the shapes of animals assigned to you.

Make the following shapes of animals:

- Bear
- Cat
- Dog
- Elephant

Checklist:

1. Is the learning material aligned with the learning objective?

2. Is the learning material aligned with the lesson plan covering the relevant concept?

3. Is the learning material clear, concise, and easy for students to understand or use?

4. Is the learning material allowing the students to develop their understanding of the concept?

5. Is the learning material incorporating conceptual or real-life connection examples that students can easily relate to?

6. Is the learning material designed to be completed in a given timeframe of the session?

If you marked [Yes] for more than 5 from the above list, it simply means that the idea will help the students acquire the knowledge.

Plan #8	
Learning objective:	To develop a kinaesthetic understanding of shapes and angles, fostering a deeper connection to geometric concepts and promoting a multi-modal approach to learning.
Taxonomy level:	Understanding
Summary of activity:	Begin the lesson by asking students what they know about the shapes and angles. Ask each student to use their hands and body to make the shapes and angles as per the instructions. Summarise the concept with some more explanation/clarification.
Grouping configuration:	Whole class – students can be asked to form shapes and angles using their hands and body.
Teaching aids/tools/resources:	

Checklist:

1. Is the planned activity aligned with the learning objective of the lesson?

2. Is the learning activity consisting of conceptual or real-life connections that will help the students understand its relevance and importance?

3. Is the learning activity working for small groups or as a whole-class activity or individually?

4. Is the learning activity providing opportunities for engaging in conceptual understanding?

5. Is the learning activity inclusive of opportunities for students to reflect on their learning and make connections to prior knowledge and experience?

6. Is the learning activity accommodating the different ability levels of the students in the classroom?

If you marked [Yes] for more than 5 from the above list, it simply means that the activity planned will work for the students.

Worksheet/ Engagement Idea #8:

Using your hands and body, form the shapes and angles as per the instructions.	
Make a square	Make an acute angle
Make a pentagon	Make an obtuse angle
Make a rectangle	Make a right-angle

Checklist:

1. Is the engagement idea aligned with the learning objective?

2. Is the engagement idea aligned with the lesson plan covering the relevant concept?

3. Is the engagement idea clear, concise, and easy for students to understand or use?

4. Is the engagement idea allowing the students to develop their understanding of the concept?

5. Is the engagement idea incorporating conceptual or real-life connection examples that students can easily relate to?

6. Is the engagement idea designed to be completed in a given timeframe of the session?

If you marked [Yes] for more than 5 from the above list, it simply means that the worksheet will help the students acquire the knowledge.

Plan #9	
Learning objective:	To demonstrate an in-depth understanding of various geometric shapes, angles, and their properties.
Taxonomy level:	Creating
Summary of activity:	Begin the lesson by asking students what they know about the shapes and angles. Give each student the materials required to work on a project assignment. Ask each student to use the materials given and make eight or ten models as per the instructions. Summarise the concept with some more explanation/ clarification.
Grouping configuration:	Individual – each student will be asked to work on a project assignment using the given materials.
Teaching aids/ tools/ resources:	Project materials

Checklist:

1. Is the planned activity aligned with the learning objective of the lesson?

2. Is the learning activity consisting of conceptual or real-life connections that will help the students understand its relevance and importance?

3. Is the learning activity working for small groups or as a whole-class activity or individually?

4. Is the learning activity providing opportunities for engaging in conceptual understanding?

5. Is the learning activity inclusive of opportunities for students to reflect on their learning and make connections to prior knowledge and experience?

6. Is the learning activity accommodating the different ability levels of the students in the classroom?

If you marked [Yes] for more than 5 from the above list, it simply means that the activity planned will work for the students.

Worksheet/Engagement Idea #9:

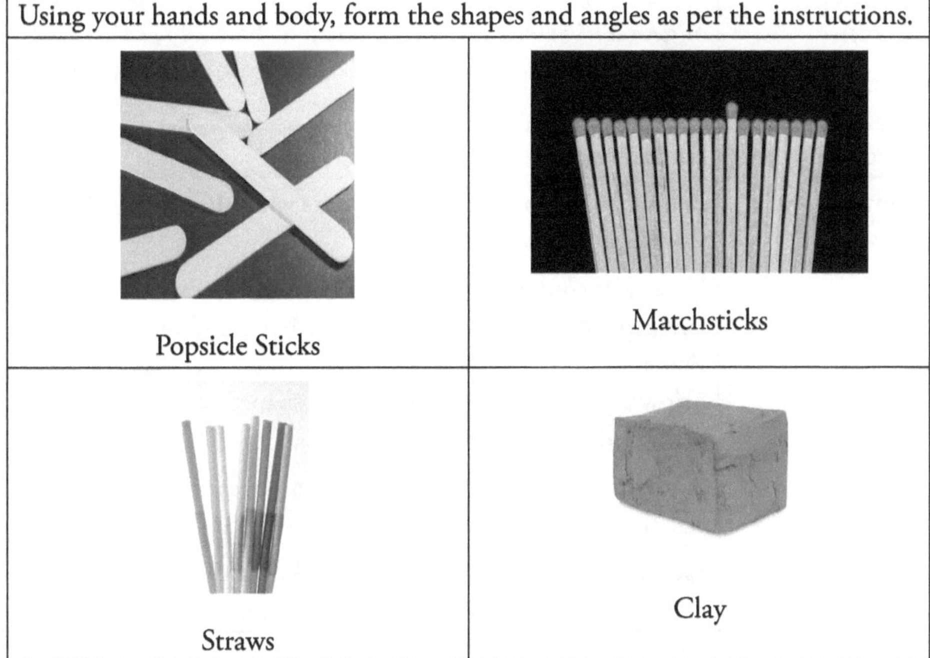

Using your hands and body, form the shapes and angles as per the instructions.

Checklist:

1. Is the learning material aligned with the learning objective?

2. Is the learning material aligned with the lesson plan covering the relevant concept?

3. Is the learning material clear, concise, and easy for students to understand or use?

4. Is the learning material allowing the students to develop their understanding of the concept?

5. Is the learning material incorporating conceptual or real-life connection examples that students can easily relate to?

6. Is the learning material designed to be completed in a given timeframe of the session?

If you marked [Yes] for more than 5 from the above list, it simply means that the idea will help students acquire the knowledge.

Plan #10	
Learning objective:	To identify shapes and angles with a deeper understanding of geometric elements within written characters, enhancing their ability to relate geometric concepts to everyday objects and textual representations.
Taxonomy level:	Understanding
Summary of activity:	Begin the lesson by asking students what they know about the shapes and angles. Give each student some alphabets from the English language. Ask them to look at each letter and identify the shapes or angles in each. Ask them to use the box given below to write the total number of shapes or angles they identified in each letter. Summarise the concept with some more explanation/ clarification.
Grouping configuration:	Individual – each student will be asked to look at the letters and identify the shapes or angles in each.
Teaching aids/ tools/ resources:	Worksheet, Letters

Checklist:

1. Is the planned activity aligned with the learning objective of the lesson?

2. Is the learning activity consisting of conceptual or real-life connections that will help the students understand its relevance and importance?

3. Is the learning activity working for small groups or as a whole-class activity or individually?

4. Is the learning activity providing opportunities for engaging in conceptual understanding?

5. Is the learning activity inclusive of opportunities for students to reflect on their learning and make connections to prior knowledge and experience?

6. Is the learning activity accommodating the different ability levels of the students in the classroom?

If you marked [Yes] for more than 5 from the above list, it simply means that the activity planned will work for the students.

Worksheet/ Engagement Idea #10:

Look at these letters and write the number of shapes or angles you identified in each.

A T L M
N W Z

Number of shapes or angles you identified in 'A'	
Number of shapes or angles you identified in 'T'	
Number of shapes or angles you identified in 'Z'	

Checklist:

1. Is the worksheet aligned with the learning objective?

2. Is the worksheet aligned with the lesson plan covering the relevant concept?

3. Is the worksheet clear, concise, and easy for students to understand or use?

4. Is the worksheet allowing the students to develop their understanding of the concept?

5. Is the worksheet incorporating conceptual or real-life connection examples that students can easily relate to?

6. Is the worksheet designed to be completed in a given timeframe of the session?

If you marked [Yes] to more than 5 from the above list, it simply means that the worksheet will help the students acquire the knowledge.

Plan #11	
Learning objective:	To accurately construct and measure various angles using clock hands, based on given instructions.
Taxonomy level:	Creating
Summary of activity:	Begin the lesson by asking students what they know about shapes and angles. Divide the students into small groups. Give each group a wall clock. Ask each group to identify the angles made due to changes in time. Summarise the concept with some more explanation/ clarification.
Grouping configuration:	Group – students will be divided into small groups. They will be given a wall clock to identify the shapes.
Teaching aids/ tools/ resources:	Wall clock

Checklist:

1. Is the planned activity aligned with the learning objective of the lesson?

2. Is the learning activity consisting of conceptual or real-life connections that will help the students understand its relevance and importance?

3. Is the learning activity working for small groups or as a whole-class activity or individually?

4. Is the learning activity providing opportunities for engaging in conceptual understanding?

5. Is the learning activity inclusive of opportunities for students to reflect on their learning and make connections to prior knowledge and experience?

6. Is the learning activity accommodating the different ability levels of the students in the classroom?

If you marked [Yes] for more than 5 from the above list, it simply means that the activity planned will work for the students.

Worksheet/ Engagement Idea #11:

<table>
<tr><td colspan="2">Identify the type of angle formed between the hands of the clock:</td></tr>
<tr><td>Type of angle: _______________</td><td></td></tr>
<tr><td>Type of angle: _______________</td><td></td></tr>
<tr><td>Type of angle: _______________</td><td></td></tr>
</table>

Checklist:

1. Is the learning material aligned with the learning objective?

2. Is the learning material aligned with the lesson plan covering the relevant concept?

3. Is the learning material clear, concise, and easy for students to understand or use?

4. Is the learning material allowing the students to develop their understanding of the concept?

5. Is the learning material incorporating conceptual or real-life connection examples that students can easily relate to?

6. Is the learning material designed to be completed in a given timeframe of the session?

If you marked [Yes] for more than 5 from the above list, it simply means that the idea will help the students acquire the knowledge.

Plan #12	
Learning objective:	To measure and construct angles accurately, demonstrating proficiency in identifying angle measurements and their geometric properties.
Taxonomy level:	Creating
Summary of activity:	Begin the lesson by asking students what they know about shapes and angles. Divide the students into small groups. Give each group a protractor. Demonstrate how to use it first. Ask each group to measure the given angles, then make the angles as per the instructions. Summarise the concept with some more explanation/ clarification.
Grouping configuration:	Group – students will be divided into small groups. They will be given protractors to measure and construct the angles.
Teaching aids/ tools/resources:	Protractor, Worksheet

Checklist:

1. Is the planned activity aligned with the learning objective of the lesson?

2. Is the learning activity consisting of conceptual or real-life connections that will help the students understand its relevance and importance?

3. Is the learning activity working for small groups or as a whole-class activity or individually?

4. Is the learning activity providing opportunities for engaging in conceptual understanding?

5. Is the learning activity inclusive of opportunities for students to reflect on their learning and make connections to prior knowledge and experience?

6. Is the learning activity accommodating the different ability levels of the students in the classroom?

If you marked [Yes] for more than 5 from the above list, it simply means that the activity planned will work for the students.

Worksheet/ Engagement Idea #12:

Use the protractor to measure and make the shapes and angles as per the instructions:	
Make an acute angle of 60 degrees	
Make an obtuse angle of 160 degrees	
Measure this shape	

Checklist:

1. Is the worksheet aligned with the learning objective?

2. Is the worksheet aligned with the lesson plan covering the relevant concept?

3. Is the worksheet clear, concise, and easy for students to understand?

4. Is the worksheet allowing the students to develop their understanding of the concept?

5. Is the worksheet incorporating conceptual or real-life connection examples that students can easily relate to?

6. Is the worksheet designed to be completed in a given timeframe of the session?

If you marked [Yes] for more than 5 from the above list, it simply means that the worksheet will help the students acquire the knowledge.

Plan #13	
Learning objective:	To independently draw various shapes and angles, demonstrating their understanding of geometric concepts.
Taxonomy level:	Applying
Summary of activity:	Begin the lesson by asking students what they know about the shapes and angles. Give each student a dotted worksheet. Ask each student to draw the shapes and angles given below. Summarise the concept with some more explanation/ clarification.
Grouping configuration:	Individual – each student will be asked to use the worksheet and draw the shapes and angles as per the instructions.
Teaching aids/ tools/ resources:	Worksheet

Checklist:

1. Is the planned activity aligned with the learning objective of the lesson?

2. Is the learning activity consisting of conceptual or real-life connections that will help the students understand its relevance and importance?

3. Is the learning activity working for small groups or as a whole-class activity or individually?

4. Is the learning activity providing opportunities for engaging in conceptual understanding?

5. Is the learning activity inclusive of opportunities for students to reflect on their learning and make connections to prior knowledge and experience?

6. Is the learning activity accommodating the different ability levels of the students in the classroom?

If you marked [Yes] for more than 5 from the above list, it simply means that the activity planned will work for the students.

Worksheet/ Engagement Idea #13:

Use the dots to draw the shapes and angles as per the instructions:
. . . .
1. Draw an acute angle 2. Draw an obtuse angle

Checklist:

1. Is the worksheet aligned with the learning objective?

2. Is the worksheet aligned with the lesson plan covering the relevant concept?

3. Is the worksheet clear, concise, and easy for students to understand or use?

4. Is the worksheet allowing the students to develop their understanding of the concept?

5. Is the worksheet incorporating conceptual or real-life connection examples that students can easily relate to?

6. Is the worksheet designed to be completed in a given timeframe of the session?

If you marked [Yes] for more than 5 from the above list, it simply means that the worksheet will help the students acquire the knowledge.

Plan #14	
Learning objective:	To accurately count the number of right angles in a given picture containing various shapes.
Taxonomy level:	Analysing
Summary of activity:	Begin the lesson by asking students what they know about shapes and angles. Divide the students into small groups. Give each group a picture. Ask each group to carefully look at the picture and identify the shapes or angles in it and write the responses in the box given below. Summarise the concept with some more explanation/ clarification.
Grouping configuration:	Group – students will be divided into small groups. They will be given pictures to identify and count the shapes or angles in them.
Teaching aids/ tools/ resources:	Picture, Worksheet

Checklist:

1. Is the planned activity aligned with the learning objective of the lesson?

2. Is the learning activity consisting of conceptual or real-life connections that will help the students understand its relevance and importance?

3. Is the learning activity working for small groups or as a whole-class activity or individually?

4. Is the learning activity providing opportunities for engaging in conceptual understanding?

5. Is the learning activity inclusive of opportunities for students to reflect on their learning and make connections to prior knowledge and experience?

6. Is the learning activity accommodating the different ability levels of the students in the classroom?

If you marked [Yes] for more than 5 from the above list, it simply means that the activity planned will work for the students.

Worksheet/ Engagement Idea #14:

Look at the picture and answer the questions given below:

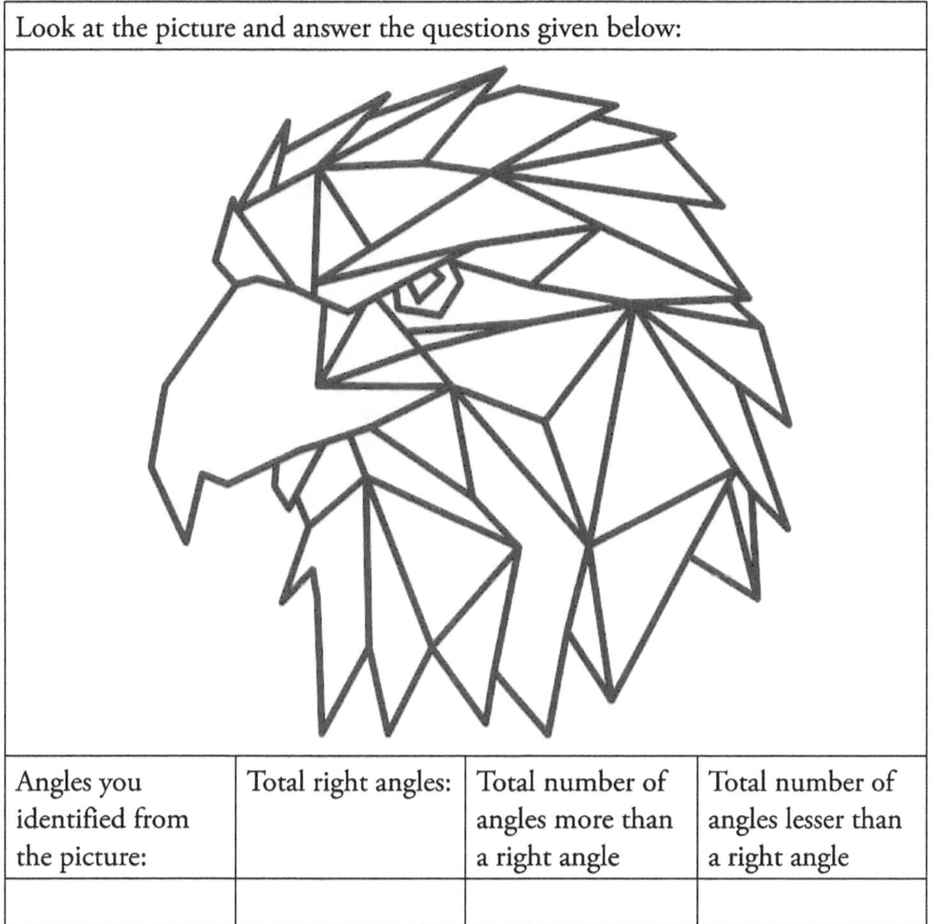

Angles you identified from the picture:	Total right angles:	Total number of angles more than a right angle	Total number of angles lesser than a right angle

Checklist:

7. Is the worksheet aligned with the learning objective?

8. Is the worksheet aligned with the lesson plan covering the relevant concept?

9. Is the worksheet clear, concise, and easy for students to understand or use?

10. Is the worksheet allowing the students to develop their understanding of the concept?

11. Is the worksheet incorporating conceptual or real-life connection examples that students can easily relate to?

12. Is the worksheet designed to be completed in a given timeframe of the session?

If you marked [Yes] for more than 5 from the above list, it simply means that the worksheet will help the students acquire the knowledge.

Plan #15	
Learning objective:	To demonstrate mastery in selecting the accurate answers pertaining to shapes and angles from provided options.
Taxonomy level:	Evaluating
Summary of activity:	Begin the lesson by asking students what they know about shapes and angles. Give each student a worksheet. Ask them to read carefully and answer the questions by choosing the most appropriate ones as per their understanding. Summarise the concept with some more explanation/ clarification.
Grouping configuration:	Individual – each student will be given a worksheet. They will be asked to carefully read and answer the questions.
Teaching aids/ tools/ resources:	Worksheet

Checklist:

1. Is the planned activity aligned with the learning objective of the lesson?

2. Is the learning activity consisting of conceptual or real-life connections that will help the students understand its relevance and importance?

3. Is the learning activity working for small groups or as a whole-class activity or individually?

4. Is the learning activity providing opportunities for engaging in conceptual understanding?

5. Is the learning activity inclusive of opportunities for students to reflect on their learning and make connections to prior knowledge and experience?

6. Is the learning activity accommodating the different ability levels of the students in the classroom?

If you marked [Yes] for more than 5 from the above list, it simply means that the activity planned will work for the students.

Worksheet/ Engagement Idea #15:

Read the questions carefully and answer them.

1. Which of the following shapes has four sides of equal length and four right angles?
 	
    a. Circle   b. Square
 	
    c. Rectangle   d. Both (b) and (c)

2. Which of the following is an acute angle?
 	
    a. 100 degrees   b. 90 degrees
 	
    c. 30 degrees   d. 360 degrees

3. How many degrees are there in a full circle?
 	
    a. 90 degrees   b. 180 degrees
 	
    c. 240 degrees   d. 360 degrees

4. The angle between the direction North and East is a/an:
 	
    a. acute angle   b. obtuse angle
 	
    c. right angle   d. reflex angle

Checklist:

1. Is the worksheet aligned with the learning objective?

2. Is the worksheet aligned with the lesson plan covering the relevant concept?

3. Is the worksheet clear, concise, and easy for students to understand or use?

4. Is the worksheet allowing the students to develop their understanding of the concept?

5. Is the worksheet incorporating conceptual or real-life connection examples that students can easily relate to?

6. Is the worksheet designed to be completed in a given timeframe of the session?

If you marked [Yes] for more than 5 from the above list, it simply means that the worksheet will help the students acquire the knowledge.

Plan #16	
Learning objective:	To accurately categorise shapes and angles based on their specific properties and characteristics
Taxonomy level:	Understanding
Summary of activity:	Begin the lesson by asking students what they know about shapes and angles. Give each student a worksheet. Ask them to look at the shapes given and categorise them as per the angles they have in each one of them. Summarise the concept with some more explanation/ clarification.
Grouping configuration:	Individual – each student will be given a worksheet. They will be asked to look at the shapes and categorise them.
Teaching aids/ tools/ resources:	Worksheet

Checklist:

1. Is the planned activity aligned with the learning objective of the lesson?

2. Is the learning activity consisting of conceptual or real-life connections that will help the students understand its relevance and importance?

3. Is the learning activity working for small groups or as a whole-class activity or individually?

4. Is the learning activity providing opportunities for engaging in conceptual understanding?

5. Is the learning activity inclusive of opportunities for students to reflect on their learning and make connections to prior knowledge and experience?

6. Is the learning activity accommodating the different ability levels of the students in the classroom?

If you marked [Yes] for more than 5 from the above list, it simply means that the activity planned will work for the students.

Worksheet/ Engagement Idea #16:

Look at the shapes given and answer the questions:

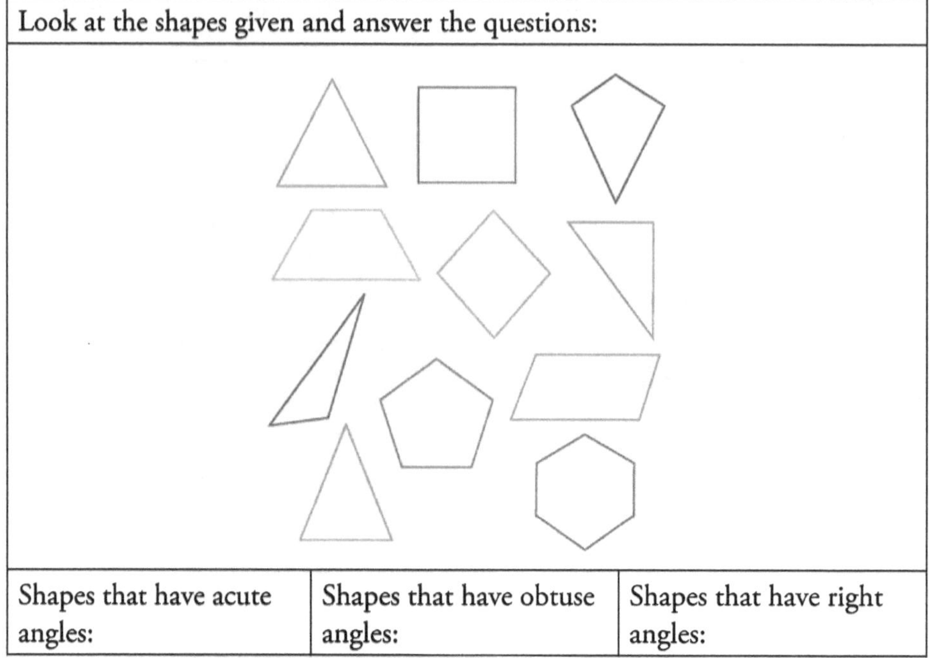

Shapes that have acute angles:	Shapes that have obtuse angles:	Shapes that have right angles:

Checklist:

1. Is the worksheet aligned with the learning objective?

2. Is the worksheet aligned with the lesson plan covering the relevant concept?

3. Is the worksheet clear, concise, and easy for students to understand or use?

4. Is the worksheet allowing the students to develop their understanding of the concept?

5. Is the worksheet incorporating conceptual or real-life connection examples that students can easily relate to?

6. Is the worksheet designed to be completed in a given timeframe of the session?

If you marked [Yes] for more than 5 from the above list, it simply means that the worksheet will help the students acquire the knowledge.

Plan #17	
Learning objective:	To demonstrate the ability to accurately draw various shapes and angles by reading and interpreting corresponding descriptions.
Taxonomy level:	Applying
Summary of activity:	Begin the lesson by asking students what they know about shapes and angles. Give each student a worksheet. Ask them to read the description given for each shape and draw them with accurate angles in the spaces given. Summarise the concept with some more explanation/ clarification.
Grouping configuration:	Individual – each student will be given a worksheet. They will be asked to read the description and draw the shapes with angles.
Teaching aids/ tools/ resources:	Worksheet

Checklist:

1. Is the planned activity aligned with the learning objective of the lesson?

2. Is the learning activity consisting of conceptual or real-life connections that will help the students understand its relevance and importance?

3. Is the learning activity working for small groups or as a whole-class activity or individually?

4. Is the learning activity providing opportunities for engaging in conceptual understanding?

5. Is the learning activity inclusive of opportunities for students to reflect on their learning and make connections to prior knowledge and experience?

6. Is the learning activity accommodating the different ability levels of the students in the classroom?

If you marked [Yes] for more than 5 from the above list, it simply means that the activity planned will work for the students.

Worksheet/ Engagement Idea #17:

Read the description given and draw the shapes with their angles.	
Draw the shapes in these columns:	**Description:**
	I have four sides. I have two pairs of equal sides. I have two pairs of equal angles. I have two pairs of parallel sides.
	I have four sides. I have two pairs of equal sides. All my angles are equal. I have two pairs of parallel sides.
	I have three sides. None of my sides or angles are equal.

Checklist:

1. Is the worksheet aligned with the learning objective?

2. Is the worksheet aligned with the lesson plan covering the relevant concept?

3. Is the worksheet clear, concise, and easy for students to understand?

4. Is the worksheet allowing the students to develop their understanding of the concept?

5. Is the worksheet incorporating conceptual or real-life connection examples that students can easily relate to?

6. Is the worksheet designed to be completed in a given timeframe of the session?

If you marked [Yes] for more than 5 from the above list, it simply means that the worksheet will help the students acquire the knowledge.

Plan #18	
Learning objective:	To analyse the physical bicycle, to identify and describe various shapes and angles present in its design, fostering a practical understanding of shapes, angles, and their applications.
Taxonomy level:	Analysing
Summary of activity:	Begin the lesson by asking students what they know about shapes and angles. Bring a bicycle to the classroom. Show it to the students. Ask the students to analyse the design of it and tell the shapes and angles they find in it. Summarise the concept with some more explanation/ clarification.
Grouping configuration:	Whole-class – they will be shown a bicycle to analyse and tell the shapes and angles they find in it.
Teaching aids/ tools/ resources:	Bicycle

Checklist:

1. Is the planned activity aligned with the learning objective of the lesson?

2. Is the learning activity consisting of conceptual or real-life connections that will help the students understand its relevance and importance?

3. Is the learning activity working for small groups or as a whole-class activity or individually?

4. Is the learning activity providing opportunities for engaging in conceptual understanding?

5. Is the learning activity inclusive of opportunities for students to reflect on their learning and make connections to prior knowledge and experience?

6. Is the learning activity accommodating the different ability levels of the students in the classroom?

If you marked [Yes] for more than 5 from the above list, it simply means that the activity planned will work for the students.

Worksheet/ Engagement Idea #18:

Look at the design of the bicycle and tell the shapes and angles you find in it.

- *How many shapes did you find on the bicycle?*
- *How many angles did you find on the bicycle?*

Checklist:

1. Is the engagement idea aligned with the learning objective?

2. Is the engagement idea aligned with the lesson plan covering the relevant concept?

3. Is the engagement idea clear, concise, and easy for students to understand or use?

4. Is the engagement idea allowing the students to develop their understanding of the concept?

5. Is the engagement idea incorporating conceptual or real-life connection examples that students can easily relate to?

6. Is the engagement idea designed to be completed in a given timeframe of the session?

If you marked [Yes] for more than 5 from the above list, it simply means that the idea will help the students acquire the knowledge.

Plan #19	
Learning objective:	To demonstrate the ability to match shapes and angles correctly to their respective options, thereby gaining proficiency in understanding geometric concepts.
Taxonomy level:	Understanding
Summary of activity:	Begin the lesson by asking students what they know about shapes and angles. Give each student a worksheet with some questions. Ask each one of them to read carefully and match them to their correct shapes and angles. Summarise the concept with some more explanation/ clarification.
Grouping configuration:	Individual – each student will be given a worksheet. They will be asked to read and match the correct options.
Teaching aids/ tools/ resources:	Worksheet

Checklist:

1. Is the planned activity aligned with the learning objective of the lesson?

2. Is the learning activity consisting of conceptual or real-life connections that will help the students understand its relevance and importance?

3. Is the learning activity working for small groups or as a whole-class activity or individually?

4. Is the learning activity providing opportunities for engaging in conceptual understanding?

5. Is the learning activity inclusive of opportunities for students to reflect on their learning and make connections to prior knowledge and experience?

6. Is the learning activity accommodating the different ability levels of the students in the classroom?

If you marked [Yes] for more than 5 from the above list, it simply means that the activity planned will work for the students.

Worksheet/ Engagement Idea #19:

Read the description given and match them to their correct shapes or angles.	
Shapes and angles	**Description:**
	I have four sides. I have two pairs of equal sides. I have two pairs of equal angles. I have two pairs of parallel sides.
	I have four sides. I have two pairs of equal sides. All my angles are equal. I have two pairs of parallel sides.
	I have three sides. None of my sides or angles are equal.

Checklist:

1. Is the worksheet aligned with the learning objective?

2. Is the worksheet aligned with the lesson plan covering the relevant concept?

3. Is the worksheet clear, concise, and easy for students to understand or use?

4. Is the worksheet allowing the students to develop their understanding of the concept?

5. Is the worksheet incorporating conceptual or real-life connection examples that students can easily relate to?

6. Is the worksheet designed to be completed in a given timeframe of the session?

If you marked [Yes] for more than 5 from the above list, it simply means that the worksheet will help the students acquire the knowledge.

Plan #20	
Learning objective:	To identify and showcase their proficiency in understanding shapes, and angles, and their application in practical problem-solving.
Taxonomy level:	Understanding
Summary of activity:	Begin the lesson by asking students what they know about shapes and angles. Give each student a worksheet with a crossword puzzle. Ask each student to read the description and solve the puzzle demonstrating their understanding. Summarise the concept with some more explanation/ clarification.
Grouping configuration:	Individual – each student will be given a worksheet. They will be asked to solve the crossword puzzle.
Teaching aids/ tools/ resources:	Crossword puzzle worksheet

Checklist:

1. Is the planned activity aligned with the learning objective of the lesson?

2. Is the learning activity consisting of conceptual or real-life connections that will help the students understand its relevance and importance?

3. Is the learning activity working for small groups or as a whole-class activity or individually?

4. Is the learning activity providing opportunities for engaging in conceptual understanding?

5. Is the learning activity inclusive of opportunities for students to reflect on their learning and make connections to prior knowledge and experience?

6. Is the learning activity accommodating the different ability levels of the students in the classroom?

If you marked [Yes] for more than 5 from the above list, it simply means that the activity planned will work for the students.

Worksheet/ Engagement Idea #20:

Read the description carefully and then solve the puzzle.

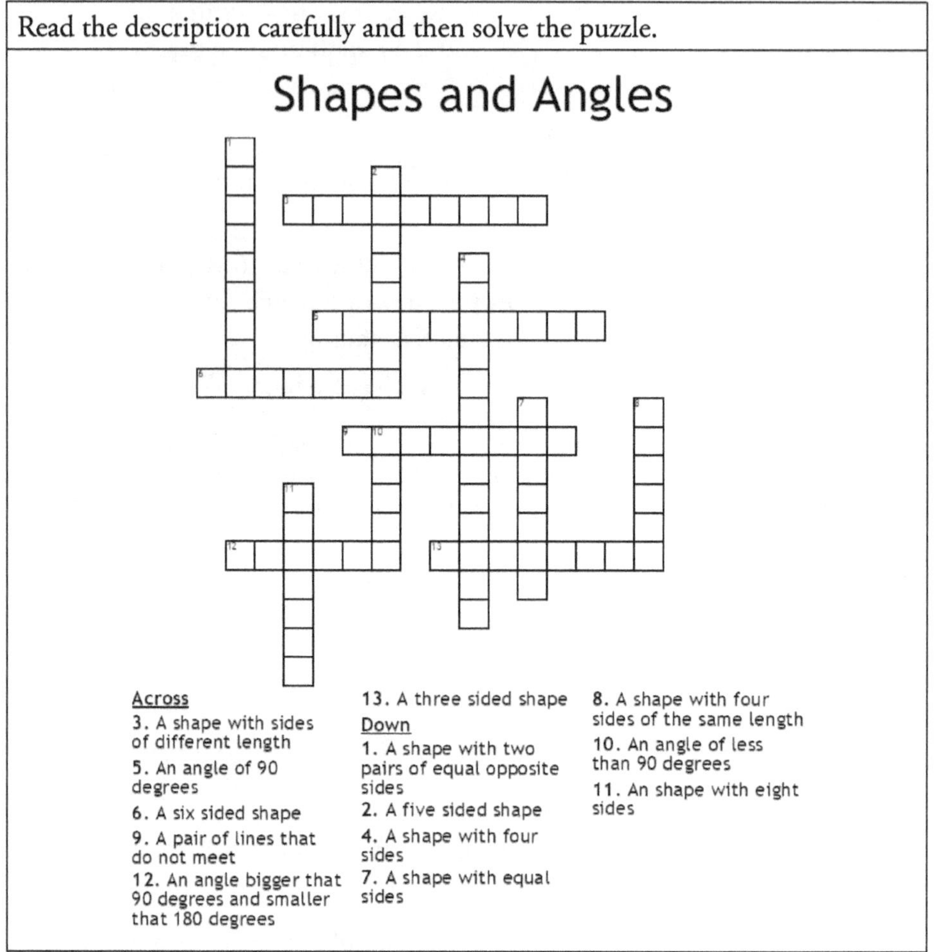

Across

3. A shape with sides of different length

5. An angle of 90 degrees

6. A six sided shape

9. A pair of lines that do not meet

12. An angle bigger that 90 degrees and smaller that 180 degrees

13. A three sided shape

Down

1. A shape with two pairs of equal opposite sides

2. A five sided shape

4. A shape with four sides

7. A shape with equal sides

8. A shape with four sides of the same length

10. An angle of less than 90 degrees

11. An shape with eight sides

Checklist:

1. Is the worksheet aligned with the learning objective?

2. Is the worksheet aligned with the lesson plan covering the relevant concept?

3. Is the worksheet clear, concise, and easy for students to understand or use?

4. Is the worksheet allowing the students to develop their understanding of the concept?

5. Is the worksheet incorporating conceptual or real-life connection examples that students can easily relate to?

6. Is the worksheet designed to be completed in a given timeframe of the session?

If you marked [Yes] for more than 5 from the above list, it simply means that the worksheet will help the students acquire the knowledge.

Plan #21	
Learning objective:	To identify and describe shapes and angles accurately with multimodal tools.
Taxonomy level:	Understanding
Summary of activity:	Begin the lesson by asking students what they know about shapes and angles. Play videos that describe the shapes and angles elaboratively. Ask each student to remember the key points from the video and tell them when asked at the end. Summarise the concept with some more explanation/ clarification.
Grouping configuration:	Whole class – A video will be played for the students. They will be asked to watch it and summarise the key points in the end.
Teaching aids/ tools/ resources:	Video, Summary worksheet.

Checklist:

1. Is the planned activity aligned with the learning objective of the lesson?

2. Is the learning activity consisting of conceptual or real-life connections that will help the students understand its relevance and importance?

3. Is the learning activity working for small groups or as a whole-class activity or individually?

4. Is the learning activity providing opportunities for engaging in conceptual understanding?

5. Is the learning activity inclusive of opportunities for students to reflect on their learning and make connections to prior knowledge and experience?

6. Is the learning activity accommodating the different ability levels of the students in the classroom?

If you marked [Yes] for more than 5 from the above list, it simply means that the activity planned will work for the students.

Worksheet/ Engagement Idea #21:

Watch the video and summarise it using the given format.

3 things I learned from the video:

1. ....

....

2. ....

....

3. ....

....

2 things I found interesting in the video:

1. ....

....

2. ....

....

1 thing I am still confused about:

1. ....

....

Checklist:

1. Is the worksheet aligned with the learning objective?

2. Is the worksheet aligned with the lesson plan covering the relevant concept?

3. Is the worksheet clear, concise, and easy for students to understand or use?

4. Is the worksheet allowing the students to develop their understanding of the concept?

5. Is the worksheet incorporating conceptual or real-life connection examples that students can easily relate to?

6. Is the worksheet designed to be completed in a given timeframe of the session?

If you marked [Yes] for more than 5 from the above list, it simply means that the worksheet will help the students acquire the knowledge.

Plan #22	
Learning objective:	To create 3D shapes and angles using the provided materials, accurately following given instructions.
Taxonomy level:	Creating
Summary of activity:	Begin the lesson by asking students what they know about shapes and angles. Divide the students into small groups. Give each group some materials. Ask each group to use the materials to make 3D shapes for each. Summarise the concept with some more explanation/ clarification.
Grouping configuration:	Group – students will be divided into small groups. They will be asked to make 3D shapes with given materials.
Teaching aids/ tools/ resources:	Straws, Popsicle sticks, Scissors, Papers, and Rubber bands.

Checklist:

1. Is the planned activity aligned with the learning objective of the lesson?

2. Is the learning activity consisting of conceptual or real-life connections that will help the students understand its relevance and importance?

3. Is the learning activity working for small groups or as a whole-class activity or individually?

4. Is the learning activity providing opportunities for engaging in conceptual understanding?

5. Is the learning activity inclusive of opportunities for students to reflect on their learning and make connections to prior knowledge and experience?

6. Is the learning activity accommodating the different ability levels of the students in the classroom?

If you marked [Yes] for more than 5 from the above list, it simply means that the activity planned will work for the students.

Worksheet/ Engagement Idea #22:

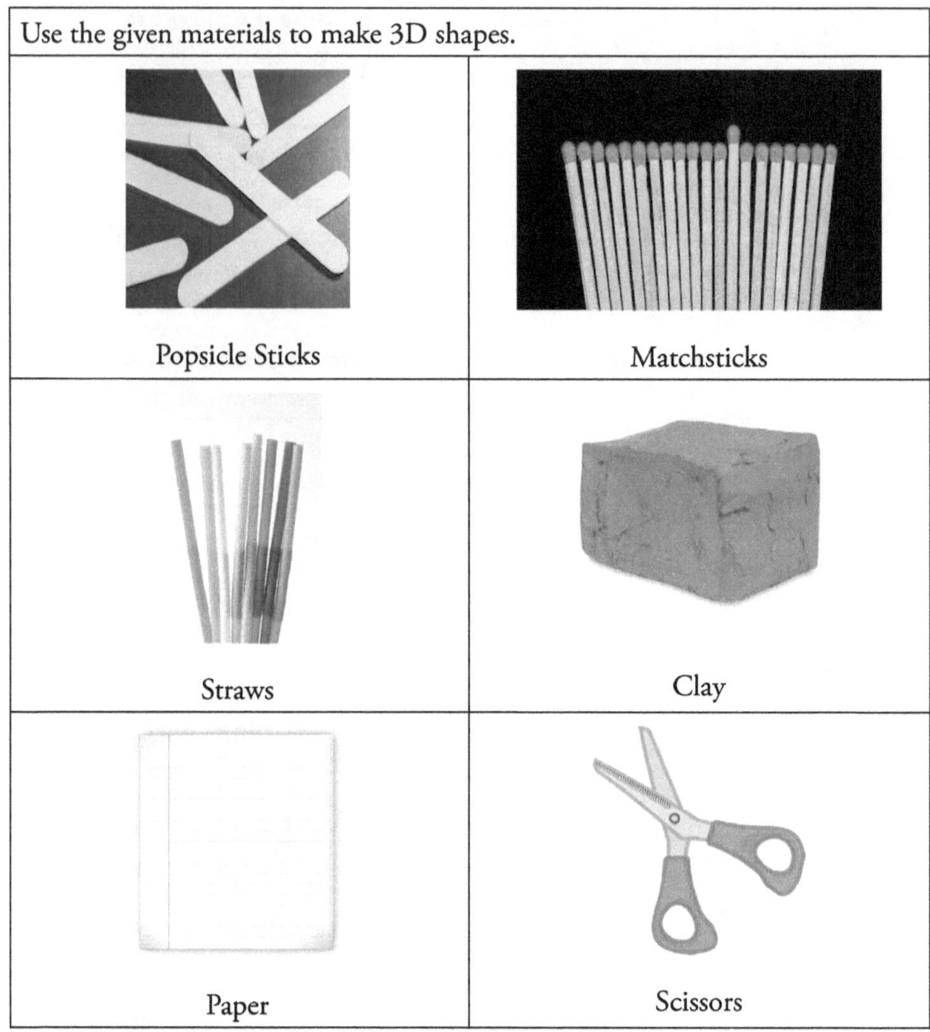

Checklist:

1. Is the learning material aligned with the learning objective?

2. Is the learning material aligned with the lesson plan covering the relevant concept?

3. Is the learning material clear, concise, and easy for students to understand?

4. Is the learning material allowing the students to develop their understanding of the concept?

5. Is the learning material incorporating conceptual or real-life connection examples that students can easily relate to?

6. Is the learning material designed to be completed in a given timeframe of the session?

If you marked [Yes] for more than 5 from the above list, it simply means that the idea will help the students acquire the knowledge.

Plan #23	
Learning objective:	To create a unique pattern of design using specific shapes and angles.
Taxonomy level:	Creating
Summary of activity:	Begin the lesson by asking students what they know about shapes and angles. Give each student some shapes on the worksheet. Ask them to design any pattern of their choice by using the shape assigned. Summarise the concept with some more explanation/ clarification.
Grouping configuration:	Individual – each student will be given a worksheet. They will be assigned a shape and asked to create a new pattern using the same shape.
Teaching aids/ tools/ resources:	Worksheet

Checklist:

1. Is the planned activity aligned with the learning objective of the lesson?

2. Is the learning activity consisting of conceptual or real-life connections that will help the students understand its relevance and importance?

3. Is the learning activity working for small groups or as a whole-class activity or individually?

4. Is the learning activity providing opportunities for engaging in conceptual understanding?

5. Is the learning activity inclusive of opportunities for students to reflect on their learning and make connections to prior knowledge and experience?

6. Is the learning activity accommodating the different ability levels of the students in the classroom?

If you marked [Yes] for more than 5 from the above list, it simply means that the activity planned will work for the students.

Worksheet/ Engagement Idea #23:

Use these shapes and angles to design patterns of your choice.	

Checklist:

1. Is the engagement idea aligned with the learning objective?

2. Is the engagement idea aligned with the lesson plan covering the relevant concept?

3. Is the engagement idea clear, concise, and easy for students to understand or use?

4. Is the engagement idea allowing the students to develop their understanding of the concept?

5. Is the engagement idea incorporating conceptual or real-life connection examples that students can easily relate to?

6. Is the engagement idea designed to be completed in a given timeframe of the session?

If you marked [Yes] for more than 5 from the above list, it simply means that the idea will help the students acquire the knowledge.

Plan #24	
Learning objective:	To accurately transform various 2D shapes into their corresponding 3D shapes by applying spatial reasoning, demonstrating a comprehensive understanding of shapes, angles, and their representation in different dimensions.
Taxonomy level:	Creating
Summary of activity:	Begin the lesson by asking students what they know about shapes and angles. Give each student some shapes on the worksheet. Ask them to transform them into 3D shapes. Summarise the concept with some more explanation/ clarification.
Grouping configuration:	Individual – each student will be given a worksheet. They will be assigned some shapes and asked to transform them into 3D shapes.
Teaching aids/ tools/ resources:	Worksheet

Checklist:

1. Is the planned activity aligned with the learning objective of the lesson?

2. Is the learning activity consisting of conceptual or real-life connections that will help the students understand its relevance and importance?

3. Is the learning activity working for small groups or as a whole-class activity or individually?

4. Is the learning activity providing opportunities for engaging in conceptual understanding?

5. Is the learning activity inclusive of opportunities for students to reflect on their learning and make connections to prior knowledge and experience?

6. Is the learning activity accommodating the different ability levels of the students in the classroom?

If you marked [Yes] for more than 5 from the above list, it simply means that the activity planned will work for the students.

Worksheet/ Engagement Idea #24:

Look at these shapes. Transform each one of them into a 3D shape.	
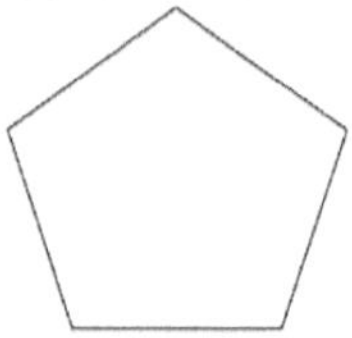	
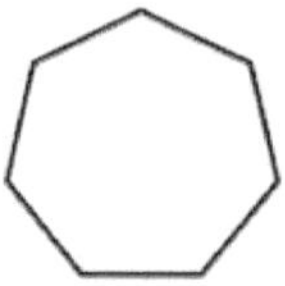	
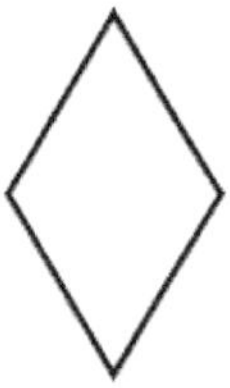	

Checklist:

1. Is the worksheet aligned with the learning objective?
2. Is the worksheet aligned with the lesson plan covering the relevant concept?
3. Is the worksheet clear, concise, and easy for students to understand or use?
4. Is the worksheet allowing the students to develop their understanding of the concept?
5. Is the worksheet incorporating conceptual or real-life connection examples that students can easily relate to?
6. Is the worksheet designed to be completed in a given timeframe of the session?

If you marked [Yes] for more than 5 from the above list, it simply means that the worksheet will help the students acquire the knowledge.

Plan #25	
Learning objective:	To demonstrate proficiency in identifying and describing various geometric shapes, their properties, and the relationships between angles through active participation and successful completion of an interactive online game focused on shapes and angles.
Taxonomy level:	Understanding
Summary of activity:	Begin the lesson by asking students what they know about the shapes and angles. Make groups of students. Ask each group to look at the online game. Explain how to play it. Ask each group to take turns and demonstrate their knowledge. Give a different game to each group. Summarise the concept with some more explanation/ clarification.
Grouping configuration:	Group – students can be divided into small groups. They can be asked to play the game assigned.
Teaching aids/ tools/ resources:	Online game

Checklist:

1. Is the planned activity aligned with the learning objective of the lesson?

2. Is the learning activity consisting of conceptual or real-life connections that will help the students understand its relevance and importance?

3. Is the learning activity working for small groups or as a whole-class activity or individually?

4. Is the learning activity providing opportunities for engaging in conceptual understanding?

5. Is the learning activity inclusive of opportunities for students to reflect on their learning and make connections to prior knowledge and experience?

6. Is the learning activity accommodating the different ability levels of the students in the classroom?

If you marked [Yes] for more than 5 from the above list, it simply means that the activity planned will work for the students.

Worksheet/ Engagement Idea #25:

<table>
<tr><td colspan="2">Look at these shapes. Transform each one of them into a 3D shape.</td></tr>
<tr><td>Link: https://www.topmarks.co.uk/ maths-games/5-7years/shapes</td><td>Scan this QR code to visit the link:</td></tr>
</table>

Checklist:

1. Is the engagement idea aligned with the learning objective?

2. Is the engagement idea aligned with the lesson plan covering the relevant concept?

3. Is the engagement idea clear, concise, and easy for students to understand or use?

4. Is the engagement idea allowing the students to develop their understanding of the concept?

5. Is the engagement idea incorporating conceptual or real-life connection examples that students can easily relate to?

6. Is the engagement idea designed to be completed in a given timeframe of the session?

If you marked [Yes] for more than 5 from the above list, it simply means that the idea will help the students acquire the knowledge.

List of plans explained:

S. no.	Plans	Bloom's Taxonomy Levels used
	To accurately recall and describe various......	Level 1
	To demonstrate proficiency in identifying......	Level 1
	To proficiently construct various shapes......	Level 2
	To identify different shapes and angles......	Level 2
	To accurately transform the given shapes......	Level 4
	To identify shapes and angles......	Level 2
	To develop a solid understanding of shapes......	Level 3
	To develop a kinesthetic understanding......	Level 2
	To demonstrate an in-depth understanding......	Level 6
	To identify shapes and angles with a......	Level 2
	To accurately construct and measure......	Level 6
	To measure and construct angles......	Level 6
	To independently draw various......	Level 3
	To accurately count the number of right angles......	Level 4
	To demonstrate mastery in selecting......	Level 5
	To accurately categorise shapes and angles......	Level 2
	To demonstrate the ability to	Level 3
	To analyse the physical bicycle......	Level 4
	To demonstrate the ability to match......	Level 2
	To identify and showcase their proficiency......	Level 2
	To identify and describe shapes......	Level 2
	To create 3D shapes and angles......	Level 6
	To create unique patterns of design......	Level 6
	To accurately transform various 2D shapes......	Level 6
	To demonstrate proficiency in identifying......	Level 2

I'm glad that you made it to this part of the book.

At this stage, I'm offering the next few pages for you to think, imagine, and practice writing the samples of lessons for the learners you have at your school. You can pick the current lesson which you are teaching or the next lesson you are about to start.

When you are done writing, I request you to take a photo of it, attach it to the email and write to me, so that I can get involved in your planning and help you in making the chosen lessons better for you. And, it is an opportunity for me to learn from you. As I said earlier in the first few pages of this book, you can be more creative than me, you can be more innovative than me, and you can be more imaginative than me. If you carefully analyse each plan for both lessons, I believe by this time you will have certain thoughts in your mind. I need you to put them down on a piece of paper and share it with me.

I have two tasks for you. Both of them are simple to do and easy to complete, yet they must come from a deeper understanding of all the prerequisites and your thorough experience from all the plans you have comprehended.

You can first write them down in the diary or notebook, then put them here in the tables given. If you choose to write here, it will become part of this book, and your thinking, planning, and imagination will also become part of this book.

And that is an honour for me, indeed.

Turn to the next page…

Task:1

Pick any lesson from the subject you teach and use the table given below to plan it as per the different taxonomy levels, keeping in mind the imagination of your learners, their cognitive capabilities, and your decision to engage them in different cognitive levels for their conceptual development.

Taxonomy level	Learning objective
Selected Lesson:	
Remembering	
Understanding	
Applying	
Analysing	
Evaluating	
Creating	

This exercise involves your planning for different cognitive levels in which you want to engage your learners for the same lesson.

Task:2

In the previous exercise, you made the planning for six cognitive levels. Here you go deeper into the planning and write ten plans to teach the same concept you chose. Previously, I gave you the levels. Here, you have the choice to pick any level(s) and plan for the same but with a minor change. You need to write the learning activities that match the taxonomy level.

Taxonomy level	Learning Activity

Now that you have written ten sample plans for a lesson, I believe you can go deeper into planning, research and use new or different techniques rigorously to find new or different plans to teach the same lesson. If you get twenty, try getting thirty. If you get thirty, try getting forty. If you get forty, try getting fifty. That's how you become a truly creative, innovative, and imaginative educator.

That's it from me!

Thank you from the bottom of my heart.

May God Bless You!

Looking forward to receiving your feedback and your planning,

Yours truly,

Amjad Razal

Write to me at: ewamjad@gmail.com

References:

1. Bloom's Taxonomy: https://www.celt.iastate.edu/instructional-strategies/effective-teaching-practices/revised-blooms-taxonomy

2. A Taxonomy for Learning, Teaching, and Assessing: a revision of Bloom's Taxonomy of educational objectives. Lorin W. Anderson, David R. Krathwohl

3. Learning Style Questionnaire: https://learning.ucmerced.edu/sites/learning.ucmerced.edu/files/page/documents/learningstyle questionnaire.pdf

4. Grade 6 NCERT Science Textbook: Lesson 'Electricity and Circuits' https://ncert.nic.in/textbook/pdf/fesc112.pdf

5. Grade 5 NCERT Math Textbook: Lesson 'Shapes and Angles' https://ncert.nic.in/textbook/pdf/eemh102.pdf